Holy Week

Proclamation 4

Aids for Interpreting
the Lessons of the Church Year

Holy Week

David L. Tiede

Series A

FORTRESS PRESS   MINNEAPOLIS

PROCLAMATION 4
Aids for Interpreting the Lessons of the Church Year
Series A—Holy Week

Library of Congress Cataloging-in-Publication Data

(Revised for vol. 1–3, Series A)

Proclamation 4.

Consists of 24 volumes in 3 series designated A, B, and C, which correspond to the cycles of the three year lectionary. Each series contains 8 basic volumes with the following titles: [1] Advent-Christmas, [2] Epiphany, [3] Lent, [4] Holy Week, [5] Easter, [6] Pentecost 1, [7] Pentecost 2, and [8] Pentecost 3. (In addition there are four volumes on the lesser festivals ᐟ
By Christopher R. Seitz
Includes bibliographies.
1. Bible—Liturgical lessons, English. 2. Bible— Homiletical use. 3. Bible—Criticism, interpretation, etc. 4. Common lectionary. 5. Church year. I. Seitz, Christopher R. II. Title: Proclamation four.
BS391.2.S37 1988   264'.34   88–10982
ISBN 0-8006-4164-7 (Series A, Holy Week).

Manufactured in the U.S.A.   AF 1–4164

93   92   91   90   89   1   2   3   4   5   6   7   8   9   10

Contents

Introduction

Holy Week is a measured march from preparation, to betrayal, to arrest, to trial, to execution, to burial, to the midnight of Easter Vigil. It is a discipline for disciples of the Lord Jesus. The slow cadences of the funeral cortege interrupt the hectic pace of life, insisting that each beat of the march be observed, step by step.

Picture a procession through Basin Street in New Orleans with the band prolonging every bar of "Just a Closer Walk with Thee." Haste will resume soon enough. Or envision a horse-drawn carriage, bearing the body of the fallen president to Arlington cemetery. The clatter of the horses' hooves and the shudder of the oversized steel rims echo in the silence far behind the Navy band. Those standing near and those far off draw together, watching in horror and fascination. What is this strange display? What befell the victim? And what will become of us?

Holy Week is a morality lesson. "Do not send to ask for whom the bell tolls," writes John Donne, "It tolls for thee." As in every observance of death, every funeral procession creeping through traffic with headlights burning, the story of Jesus' passion is a reminder: "In the midst of life, we are in death." The rhythm and the ritual arrest our attention. The way of the cross is the human story of the inevitable approach of death. "So teach us to number our days, O Lord. Give us time for amendment of life." Too soon the sleep of death will overtake us whether with a crashing blow, a failure of frail flesh, an anguished cry of despair, or a painful humiliation of betrayal. Too soon our "summons comes to join that innumerable caravan which moves to that mysterious realm" (William Cullen Bryant, *Thanatopsis*). Every child who views the stations of the cross, moving from one to another around an old chancel begins to understand: This strange and terrible story is about *me*.

Holy Week is also about love and justice. The passion narrative could never be cold or fatalistic. The agents in the narrative are engaged in a struggle of wills. Jesus' impending death looms as inescapable, even necessary. But such necessity is more than a reminder of mortality. It is a revelation of the powers and institutions which oppose Jesus' reign of mercy and justice. Jesus' death and life have public consequences for the participants and readers of the story. Knowing that Jesus will surely die does not produce despair or resignation. This is a story of courage and obedience, inspiring the faithful to renewed commitment to God's saving purpose in this contested world.

Holy Week is finally a story about God. More than a morality play or a tragic drama, this is a gospel story. It is "Holy Week" because God is at work even in its dire disclosures of human sin and tragic blindness.

God's saving activity is far from evident from the Sunday of the Passion through the dark night of the Easter Vigil. A gifted prophet marches to his death. Does he not see what is coming? A sinful humanity executes the Lord of glory? Why do they not understand the terrible consequences? The gospel story is obscured by the power of death and the apparent dominance of Jesus' adversaries. Even the eye of faith must strain to see that within the violence and pathos of Holy Week, God is accomplishing the saving purpose for which the Messiah was sent.

The Scripture readings for Holy Week are drumbeats, measuring the march to Jesus' death. They are often complex passages, surprisingly long, and not always synchronized. They are read as a litany of lamentation. They regulate the rhythm of contemplation. Day by day, the ritual of Holy Week is paced by these unhurried readings.

They are also floodlights, illuminating the tragic stage of human history. The truth must be told, even if it is painful to hear. Humanity's willful resistance to God's justice and mercy must be revealed. Our denial and self-deception will only perpetuate the blindness and defiance in the story. We read these passages day by day as an exercise in repentance. All illusions of our righteousness fade away under the bright lamp of truth. Our sinful plight is disclosed.

These readings for Holy Week, however, are also testimonies to the gospel truth with its saving promise for humanity and the world. The triumph of Jesus' reign lies ahead in Easter, and signs of that hope will be given even in the midst of this story. Even the depth of the disclosure of human sin is a sign of scriptural confidence in the grandeur of God's salvation. Holy Week reveals the great gap between God's holiness and human sin. Even as testimonies to God's grace, these passages refuse to indulge any denial of the realities of death and sin.

The interpreter of the Scriptures of Holy Week is a teacher, truth teller, and proclaimer. Few communities of faith will observe all of these days. Perhaps some congregations will prepare devotional resources for home use. Many leaders will be so busy during the week that they will find it difficult even to read the assigned Scriptures. Nevertheless, the long-standing tradition of Holy Week provides a unique setting for ministry.

The rituals and rhythms of the week provide an opportunity for people to experience heightened awareness of life and death with Christ. Such devotional discipline in turn may increase our readiness to hear the tragic truth of our human situation and the word of salvation which God declares. Methodical study of this special daily lectionary is therefore an act of ministry, introducing the interpreter and the people to the scriptural rhythms of the week and setting a context for the proclamation of repentance and salvation.

Sunday of the Passion
Palm Sunday

Lutheran	Roman Catholic	Episcopal	Common Lectionary
Isa. 50:4-9a	Isa. 50:4-7	Isa. 45:21-25	Isa. 50:4-9a
Phil. 2:5-11	Phil. 2:6-11	Phil. 2:5-11	Phil. 2:5-11
Matt. 26:1—27:66	Matt. 26:14—27:66	Matt. 27:1-54	Matt. 26:14—27:66 or Matt. 27:11-54

Collect: Almighty God, you sent your Son, our Savior Jesus Christ, to take our flesh upon him and to suffer death on the cross. Grant that we may share in his obedience to your will and in the glorious victory of his resurrection, through your Son, Jesus Christ our Lord, who lives and reigns with you and the Holy Spirit, one God, now and forever. Amen.

The long-standing identification of this day as "Palm Sunday" may overshadow the beginning of Holy Week. None of the lectionaries for Holy Week in Year A include the story of Jesus' entry into Jerusalem (Matt. 21:1-9), but many churches use it to open the service. Outlines of the gospels also traditionally identify the entry as the beginning of Jesus' "last week in Jerusalem" (Matt. 21:1—27:66; Mark 11:1—15:47; Luke 19:28—23:56).

The palm fronds have long signaled one of the great events for congregational celebration, and the story of Jesus' entry into Jerusalem must be read if the procession and hymns are to make any sense. The triumphal entry is great church drama in any case, and every child can wave the palm out of the car window on the way home. And next week, there will be new clothes, egg hunts, and Easter bunnies. If that family observes only the triumphal procession one Sunday and the resurrection the next, all of the unpleasantness of Holy Week can be completely avoided.

Which is exactly the problem. A society that prefers to deny the reality of sin and death may love Palm Sunday and Easter. Then the passion of the Messiah and the severity of Holy Week may be discounted as negative or masochistic or unhealthy. One critic of theologies of the cross has said, "I am tired of churches that spend all year waiting for Good Friday." He wanted nothing to do with the harsh realities of betrayal, trial, execution, and burial. But without them, what is the meaning of Easter? What is the message of the resurrection without the crucifixion in all of its historical and human complexity?

Those who are willing to settle for the delights of bunnies and egg hunts don't need the Christian faith at all, which is why so many insipid greeting cards of the season are filled with pagan themes of agricultural renewal. Of course Christians also rejoice at fertility and the renewing power of nature at springtime. But these are pleasant cures for mild conditions, not the gospel of Jesus Christ. Rituals of seasonal renewal cannot touch the depth of human need for salvation from sin, death, and the powers of evil. Only the gospel of Jesus' death and resurrection is adequate to such realities.

Holy Week is an affirmation of joy, grounded in faith. It is a discipline of the church whereby the power of the word of God to kill and make alive is unleashed among the faithful.

The problem is posed sharply on this Sunday. The triumphal procession may open the service, but then the texts press further. In his royal entry, Jesus lays down a gauntlet. This Messiah intends something. He is not a deluded royal pretender parading into Jerusalem to be liquidated by the efficient Romans. He poses a larger challenge. He enacts the distinctive reign of God, to the surprise and confusion of those around him as well as to the disdain of the authorities in Jerusalem. His entry may be dramatic, but it is only imposing for those who know his mission. So also, his resurrection a week later is no vague myth of human persistence. The substance of these glorious displays is disclosed in the depth and discipline of Holy Week.

The lectionary for the day drives to this point. This may be Palm Sunday, but it is also the Sunday of the Passion. This day is the portal to the difficult and wondrous way of the cross of the Messiah Jesus. Once the procession is concluded, the lessons lead the faithful into the divine drama that lies within the external display. This parade will end in an execution, and that travesty of justice will prove to be God's means of salvation for all the world.

FIRST LESSON: ISAIAH 50:4-9a

Text: The verses from Isaiah (Roman Catholic 50:4-7) quickly shift the tone from the praise of the triumphal entry. As in Isaiah 45:21-25 (Episcopal lectionary), the prophet declares God to be an actor in history, an agent who calls humanity into court. The real time of human life and events is an arena where God is at work, establishing dominion and contesting human claims to righteousness. In this world of claims and counterclaims, God convenes the court to determine righteousness. It is God who summons the people and the nations, "Declare and present your case!" (45:21), but it is God's testimony to the truth that will prevail.

This scene is graphic, picturing the nations of the world putting God on trial. But then God turns the case around and stands with the accused servant. Then and now, God offends humanity by not submitting to our judgment, and the modern world is especially shocked by a God who means business. "Just who do you think you are?" ask the proud who are accustomed to judging. We think God is on the defensive. But the prophet insists that God challenges humanity and brings us into court. God refuses to be reduced to the scale of our idols.

In Isaiah 50, God's way of engaging humanity appears weak. God asks the questions that reveal knowledge of presumptuous human charges: "Is my hand shortened, that it cannot redeem? Or have I no power to deliver?" (50:2). God refuses to accept our definitions of power and glory, to be judged on the terms established by the "high and mighty." Those who think that God is weak simply have no understanding of the hidden strength of divine will and righteousness.

Verses 4-11 are often identified as the third servant song of chaps. 40–55. While the lectionaries are not identical, the testimony of this witness is astonishing in each version. This servant tells the truth about God in the court of world opinion and takes abuse for faithfulness. Having been given "the tongue of those who are taught," that is, taught by God, the messenger still has no illusions that people are eager to hear God's word and will.

Proclamation: This servant is God's embodied message. God is not obliged to take on the world in a show of strength. Even the messenger's apparent weakness is a sign of divine restraint. But the servant bears the truth and knows its authority. Under the commission of this word, the servant sets his "face like a flint" (see Luke 9:51, 53), adamant that God's word of deliverance will be vindicated.

The motif of vindication is crucial. The reputation of the messenger is at stake. But more critically, God's reputation is at stake, and God's righteousness is on the line in the person and message of this witness. This divine messenger understands that God has made a human both the medium and the message. The prophet instructs the reader not to judge God by what the world requires of divinity. God has adopted a stunning strategy. God has put human presumption in the dock and sent an unlikely messenger to convey and represent divine will and righteousness.

The world idolizes people of power and influence. The high and mighty are regularly judged by a different standard. When the faithful find themselves at odds with those who run the world, they appear weak, foolish, and perhaps subversive. That story has been told repeatedly in Christian history. But then who is their judge? Where is God when the opinion makers in the company, high school, or government turn against you? How can the true God be distinguished from the idol, especially when so many people admire or even worship wealth, splendor, and influence? Isaiah's message is directed exactly at such concerns.

Christian readers have long seen the servant as a prototype of Jesus. God did a new thing in Jesus, to be sure, but God acted consistently with prophetic declarations. Those who insist on a more positive and glorious religion may be fond of palm processions and Easter trumpets, but they may want none of this repentance. They may also have a glorious god, but the God whose holiness confronts us in Holy Week may offend their sensibilities. This God perfects power in humility, relying upon weak human witnesses to be vindicated in the public arena, and conferring divine authority on mere mortals. Now such peculiar strength and power will be the way that the triumphant Jesus will enact the kingdom acclaimed with palms.

EPISTLE: PHILIPPIANS 2:5-11

Text: The early Christian hymn in Philippians 2 declares the same divine program as the servant songs of Isaiah. The logic and praise lead to the same astonishing revelation: God's way of dominion is fulfilled in humiliation. This strength can only be worshiped. It is too wondrous for mere mortals.

Scholars usually identify v. 6 as the beginning of the hymn. The RSV still displays the seam where an older memory piece with poetic structure begins. The relative pronoun *who* introduces a series of phrases that summarize the passion story in a closely knit confession of faith. These statements are not merely descriptive identifications of Jesus. They are declarations of what Jesus' death meant with respect to his relationship to God as Messiah and Lord. The gospel story is not merely a factual account of Jesus' death. It is a revelation that what Jesus did and how he died were fundamental to how God rules.

This understanding of Jesus' death predates the New Testament, since Paul is reciting words which had become traditional before he wrote his letters. These verses provided later Greek theologians with the basis of their understanding of the *kenosis* or "emptying" of Jesus' divine nature. Perhaps this very early Christian memory piece did not arise from such complex theological reflection, but it did clearly indicate that Jesus' humiliation and death were directly connected with the meaning of his resurrection and glorification: "Therefore God has highly exalted him." Jesus' death was not an unfortunate accident on the way to his glory.

This is what God had in mind all along, from before Jesus' birth. Relinquishing "divine right" was unthinkable for the kings of Europe. This messiah relinquished "equality with God" that others would have "grasped" or "seized" for personal advantage. But Jesus' obedience unto death had the welfare and salvation of mortal humanity in view. The supreme power of the universe is foregone for the sake of identification with human beings.

In the first century, this revelation was also a mighty political commentary. The emperor Caligula claimed divine prerogatives and privileges for himself around the year 40. Those who opposed him, including many in Israel, faced mortal peril. The large egos of the political theologies of the empire always claimed divine authority in the name of the Roman order. Sometimes they also "grasped" for recognition as gods, even before they were acclaimed divine at death. They seemed to have the power of heaven on their side. But like Isaiah, the early Christians said "No." Caesar's dominion did not make him "Lord and God and Savior," as he claimed. God's reign is perfected in the humble obedience of the servant.

Proclamation: This revelation is highly significant for modern times. Only a few mad rulers of this century may have claimed direct divine status for themselves, but all tyrants declare that God or destiny or history is on their side. Their clout is its own testimony. The innocent who stand in the way are disregarded as "naive" or "in league with the enemy" and "worthless."

The central point of this ancient Christian hymn is a christological or messianic revelation. It is a disclosure of how God's ultimate rule works. Might does not make right in the kingdom of God. Rather, the innocent sufferings of Jesus transform the hollow stares of the victims of grand human systems into a mirror of God's reign. The ideologies, economic systems, and imperial personalities promising salvation are revealed to deliver misery. Suffering is not glorified, so that we should seek it; but it is redeemed. The Messiah has been there. The ultimate violence of disregard for the dignity of those who suffer is exposed. Christ Jesus has vindicated their worth by his own sufferings.

Paul cites this hymn to make an ethical point. In this chapter, Paul appeals to the Christians to deal with each other in love and reconciliation. Some Christians appreciate the christological point of the hymn but pull back from its moral claim. Others are attracted to its plea for Christian behavior but are disinterested in its revelation about the relationship between Jesus and God before Jesus' birth and after his resurrection. Yet the unity of these emphases or usages must be preserved.

These verses do not indulge in speculation about God and the Trinity. They are a revelation of God's love and the purpose of Jesus' mission. They explore the economy of the Trinity in terms of the dynamic relationship between God's will and Jesus' mission. We do not know everything about the unity and complexity of the Trinity. This is the hymnic language of praise, not analytic description. But we now know enough to grasp the hidden strength of God at work in the saving obedience of Jesus, and we understand that this is the economy of the kingdom. And what a way to run a kingdom it is!

GOSPEL: MATTHEW 26:1—27:66

Text: This passage is an immensely long reading. Its 141 verses reach far beyond even the long reading from John for Good Friday (see below). This narrative is a text to be savored as it is read with care and cadence. It is not a passage which should be turned over to the youth group for public reading. It requires exceptional discipline and maturity to read this passion narrative aloud.

In the late nineteenth century, scholars noted that the passion narratives had unusual coherence. Preoccupied with questions of historical verifiability, they focused on these narratives as records of the events of Jesus' last days. They observed that the three synoptic gospels diverged on details and even on smaller matters of sequence, but they still stressed the narratives' factual character.

Of course these passages are historical records, and they are much more complete in detail and fact than the accounts of the death of any other ancient figure, including Socrates' death as told by Plato. But the narrative quality of the story is more fundamentally a sign of its literary quality than a mark of its historical accuracy. The structure and poetry of the story arise from a faith that yearns to be communicated through a story of a brutal execution. This is a tale well told to convey a truth so large that the brute facts strain under the weight of meaning. This story was meant to be read aloud, with drama and suspense.

The reader should be aware of two aspects of the narrative: 1. the rich complexity of the characters in the story; and 2. the profound irony that Jesus is executed for being who he truly is, "the King of the Jews, the Christ, the Son of God."

In *Matthew as Story* (Minneapolis: Fortress Press, 1988 [2nd ed.]), Jack Dean Kingsbury notes that Jesus and the disciples are full or "round" characters in the narrative while the religious leaders are "flat" with fewer dimensions. The story also includes "stock" characters such as the woman in the house of Simon (27:6-13). The drama and movement in the passion narrative revolve around complex interactions among Jesus, his disciples, and his adversaries in the midst of their unswerving drive to kill him.

Chapter 26 is especially full of insights into the characters. Jesus knows what lies ahead, and his predictions punctuate the story (26:2, 13, 18, 21, 29, 31, 34, 45-46, 64). His way to death reveals obedience to the will of God in fulfillment of the Scriptures (26:39, 56). He is not a tragic figure who is ignorant or blind, but neither is he cool or detached as one who merely played a role would be. His dialogue with Judas (26:20-25, 48-50) is pained because friendship has turned to betrayal. His warnings to Peter (26:30-35, 40-41) are fulfilled in bitter tears (56, 69-75). Even his words to the crowds at his arrest are filled with the pathos of their blindness and his obedience (26:55-56).

Judas is a complex and haunting character in Matthew's narrative (see the lesson from Matt. 26:14-25 for Wednesday below). He seeks out the chief priests, apparently motivated by greed (26:14-16). Confronted by Jesus at the supper, he is warned in the sharpest terms possible of the fate of the betrayer (26:20-25). Without the reader knowing of his departure (see John 13:30), Judas is heralded as the arriving betrayer by Jesus in Gethsemane (26:46) and hailed by Jesus as "Friend" (26:48-50). Only after the betrayal of this friend leads to Jesus' condemnation does Judas have a change of heart. He confesses his sin, receives no absolution from the chief priests, throws down the money, and hangs himself. His only epitaph is the potter's field, fulfilling the Scriptures in a curse.

Peter's character is the most well-rounded of the disciples. The episodes of his eager promises (26:33-35), sleeping on watch (vv. 40, 43, 45), and flight (v. 56) reach a climax in his return to the courtyard of the high priest (vv. 69-75). Once more he was probably trying to be faithful to his promises, but Jesus' predictions come true, all too literally. Peter's is a story of failure and denial, not betrayal. It is a subplot, filled with human pathos. The remorse of failed faithfulness is a powerful theme of Holy Week.

Chapter 27 moves to the larger public arena, expanding the dire irony that Jesus is being killed for claiming to be who he actually is. If he were merely a pretender, his death has no great consequence. But if his accusers grasp at all with whom they are dealing, their condemnations are self-incriminating. Pilate is the only character who nearly rises from the flat page when he "wondered greatly" at Jesus' silence and when his wife warned him of her dream (27:14, 18-19), but he washes his hands and slips back into the plane of tragic ignorance and violence, delivering Jesus to die.

Proclamation: The cries for the death of "the King of the Jews" and "the Son of God" are shrill on the lips of Jesus' accusers, but they are full of meaning for the Christian reader. Those who watch the scene from here must, like Pilate, "wonder greatly" at such human blindness and insight. And the greater mystery is not whether the accusers were acting and speaking "out of envy" (v. 18), or mockery (vv. 29, 41), or derision (vv. 39, 44). But what does it mean that "He trusts in God"? Both the mockers (v. 43) and the Messiah (v. 46) know that this is the issue.

The Passion Narrative explores the human story surrounding Jesus, because it is a story of judgment and salvation for humanity. It also drives to the truth of the charges against Jesus so that when he dies the verdict is final. "Truly this was the Son of God!" (27:54).

Then the question of God's will and reign becomes all the more urgent. This is the question of Holy Week, and the Gospels are confident of the answer. But the evangelist refuses to simplify either the question or the answer. The whole story must be told so that step by step the faithful may be instructed in the wondrous and strong ways of God in judgment and in mercy.

The preacher must also resist easy answers and instant relevance. The long readings invite meditation, focusing upon the story itself, allowing the evangelist's telling to do its work. If the hearers are drawn into the sacred drama, captured by the plight of Peter, shocked by Judas' betrayal, offended by Pilate's disdain, the sermon will have been faithful to the text.

Those who struggle with God's will in the midst of illness, disappointment, or shame will be glad to move slowly through this awesome story. They are already weary of instant remedies. The deepest mysteries of life and death are probed here, and shallow explanations will not satisfy.

But the confidence of the evangelist will also be evident, and the preacher also knows that God's salvation is more than adequate to the most devastating human sin and suffering. This is why a long story of unjust condemnation and execution belongs in Holy Week. The holiness of God is being perfected in the midst of human violence and complicity, and the cost is high. Christians dare face the dire truth about themselves and the world in the story of Jesus' death without flinching or denial because here the measure of God's love and forgiveness is disclosed.

Monday in Holy Week

Lutheran	Roman Catholic	Episcopal	Common Lectionary
Isa. 42:1-9	Isa. 42:1-7	Isa. 42:1-9	Isa. 42:1-9
Heb. 9:11-15		Heb. 11:39—12:3	Heb. 9:11-15
John 12:1-11	John 12:1-11	John 12:1-11 *or* Mark 14:3-9	John 12:1-11

Collect for Monday in Holy Week: O God, your Son chose the path which led to pain before joy and the cross before glory. Plant his cross in our hearts, so that in its power and love we may come at last to joy and glory; through your Son, Jesus Christ our Lord. Amen.

The readings for Monday, Tuesday, and Wednesday of Holy Week will certainly receive less public attention throughout the church, but they are treasuries of disclosure of God's gracious reign in a defiant world. The preacher will do well to devote thought and prayer to as many of the passages as possible.

Each text has its own contours and contexts. In the frame of Holy Week, these readings form a collage for meditation. The central figure is constant: Jesus on his way to death and dominion. And all around him, the testimonies, tales, and hymns of many human occasions open the eyes of the reader and proclaimer. God's way of saving rule is strange and wonderful.

FIRST LESSON: ISAIAH 42:1-9

Text: These verses include the first of the "servant songs" (42:1-4, see also 49:1-6, Tuesday in Holy Week; 50:4-11, Wednesday; and 52:13—53:12, Holy Thursday) of Isaiah 40–55 coupled with an oracle of God's righteous reign in history (42:5-9). Modern interpreters have often spoken of the "suffering servant" songs of II Isaiah, and first-century Christians were already probing these verses for an understanding of Jesus' humiliation and reign.

But this text says nothing about suffering. Verses 1-4 state the public commission of God's servant, and vv. 5-9 pronounce God's rule of justice in the world through chosen Israel. The gentleness of the servant's mandate is clear (vv. 2-3). This is not a propaganda campaign or a power move that will crush the weak or quench faint spirits. But the servant will persist until God's objective is achieved (v. 4). The entire passage is a strong affirmation of confidence in God's rule, not a theology of suffering.

The focal point of the servant's commission is to "bring forth" or "establish *justice*" (Heb. *mishpat*, vv. 2, 3, and 4). God's will and mission is justice, and the word summarizes God's whole purpose in choosing a beloved servant for the task. Those who hold a host of convictions and notions about "justice" and "love" will be tempted to seize these verses for their agenda or ideologies. But these chapters in Isaiah fill the word "justice" with new content. The prophet will settle for nothing less than the entire law of God (v. 4), the restoration of Israel, and the new order of God's rule as savior and redeemer (vv. 42-43, 49).

God's reign and means of achieving "law and order" challenge and transform popular conceptions. God is the one who teaches "the path of justice," and God's rule "brings princes to nought, and makes the rulers of the earth as nothing" (40:14, 23). The servant is authorized with God's Spirit, and his is a mission extending God's justice beyond Israel, to the "gentiles" (RSV: nations, v. 1), the earth, and the coastlands (v. 4).

This is one of the great "mission of God" (*missio dei*) texts of Isaiah 40–55. It is filled with the vision of the exilic prophet that God's Spirit was stirring to accomplish a new thing. Israel's return to Palestine was only part of the divine design. This song focuses upon the servant, who may have been a charismatic leader, a new Moses, or Israel personified. Above all, the text envisions God's agency of salvation and justice exercised through the human servant, beloved of God.

In vv. 5-9, God links the commission of the servant to Israel's calling. This is God the creator speaking (vv. 5 and 8), not some petty idol (see Isaiah 40:12-13, 44:9-20). The servant's commission to bring forth justice (vv. 1-4) is now expounded as Israel's call to be "a covenant to the people, a light to the nations." The illumination of God's justice will be a miraculous blessing to all the peoples of the world. The righteousness of God is now revealed in Israel's role as this covenant and light. God's "justice" is an active, saving mission in the world.

Proclamation: The historical occasion of Israel in exile is not identical to that of a modern community of faith on the Monday of Holy Week, and the proclaimer must declare God's "justice" anew. By their declarative form, however, these verses are proclamation in a new context as soon as they are read. This is the "word of God" in its direct address, and the hearer is immediately brought into the broad world of God's saving purposes. God's commission addresses "you" who are called to be a light to the nations.

This confident mission sets the proper context for the trials and suffering of Holy Week. God's mission is not misery, although suffering will certainly follow in the world as it is. God's purpose is salvation, not enslavement, and the ways that God will accomplish this plan are consistent with its content of God's justice perfected in mercy.

The story of Jesus' final week in Jerusalem is filled with conflict over legitimate authority, political intrigue, and betrayal. This is a highly particular narrative, told in real time. By comparison, Isaiah's grand proclamations may seem abstract or unreal.

But these songs and oracles were also filled with challenge to the political and theological claims of the empires of the world. They declared from of old that God was about to confront the world with a justice that would expose the darkness of all such claims of the high and mighty. Read in the context of Holy Week, Isaiah's testimony reveals the persistence and triumph which God perfected through the passion of the servant Jesus.

EPISTLE: HEBREWS 9:11-15

Text: This passage leads the reader and hearer into the complex world of sacrificial practices in Israel. Since the date, place, and authorship of Hebrews can only be estimated from the text, interpreters debate the author's knowledge and attitude toward the temple which stood in Jerusalem until it was destroyed by the Romans in 70 C.E. Hebrews may well originate from a Jewish circle which regarded the Jerusalem temple as inferior long before some of them ever heard of Jesus or became Christians.

Jewish philosophers like Philo of Alexandria probably would have appreciated Hebrews' emphasis on the perfection of the heavenly sanctuary "not made with hands" (9:24) compared to the limited "earthly sanctuary" (9:1, 11). These Jews and Jewish Christians often shared a distinct priestly understanding of the link between heaven and earth. In contrast to the prophetic view of Isaiah 40–55 where history is an arena of divine justice, the priestly world of Hebrews envisions a sacred canopy stretched between heaven and earth. What happens in the earthly sanctuary is but a shadow of the perfect heavenly reality. The efficacy of earthly sacrifice awaits heavenly enactment. The real world is transcendent, as is God. Much will be said about purity to serve in God's presence, but little about God as an actor in history.

This text, therefore, paints a complex picture of Jesus as the mediator of a new covenant. Christ has a unique status as God's Son (see Heb. 4:14-16; 5:5-7 for Good Friday). His flesh and blood are the means of entry into the true heavenly sanctuary, through the veil of the sacred canopy that separates heaven and earth (see 10:19-20). The old earthly covenant of sacrifice and the Mosaic tent was but "a copy and shadow of the heavenly sanctuary" (8:5). Now a new priestly people and covenant have been established through Jesus' death.

The logic of the passage is consistently a move "from the lesser to the greater." If the first covenant availed to some extent, "how much more" efficacious shall be the covenant sealed with the blood of Christ. If the earthly temple was a temporal symbol or shadow, how much more real, perfect, and enduring is the heavenly Holy Place. The contrast clearly implies the great superiority of the "new covenant," but the symbolic authenticity of the first covenant is essential to understanding Jesus' death as a sacrifice for sin. Jewish temple rituals were reflections of heavenly realities, and Jesus' death has broken through to accomplish redemption in the heavenly Holy Place itself (9:12).

Proclamation: In preaching on Hebrews, it is tempting to deny the reality of the created order, and it is distressingly easy to turn Christian preaching into anti-Judaism. Both of these dangers must be consciously avoided because they are unfaithful to the text as well as poor Christian theology. Hebrews compels the preacher to struggle with Jesus' death in the flesh and in Jewish history. Those who might be content to discuss symbol systems and ritual must come to terms with the scandal of the incarnation in all of its historical particularity.

Every era has its religions that promise escape to the heavenly realm. The Platonism of the Hellenistic age had reached into the soul of Judaism and lured many early Christians into schemes of salvation that denied the reality of this world. But the Book of Hebrews turns such cosmic speculation into a stage for the incarnation of the Son of God. No rituals of immortality for souls striving for perfection are allowed.

The blood and death of Jesus Christ proves to be God's venture to reach into the earthly realm. Jesus' death effected a new covenant in full obedience to the will of God. "By a single offering he has perfected for all time those who are sanctified" (10:14). The way through the curtain of the Holy Place (9:12) proves to be through Jesus' blood and flesh (10:19-20).

Such particularity is scandalous and unrepeatable. Israel's history of repeatable sacrifices is not demeaned by this sacrifice. It is redeemed, fulfilled. The author of Hebrews is not on the same frequency as the prophet or Isaiah 40–55, but they agree at the most profound level. The proclaimer of the "word of God" must drive to this basic insight. God has surprised the politicians of the world with their theological claims and the philosophers with their ideologies of transcendence. In the flesh and blood of Jesus, God has proved to be the one who cares for mere mortals. The whole story of Jesus, the epic of Holy Week, is a disclosure of God's determination to save us. That is what Israel's prior history discloses about God, and now it has been proved in flesh and blood in Jesus.

GOSPEL: JOHN 12:1-11

Text: John's version of the story of the woman who anointed Jesus provides a quiet interlude in a dangerous series of events. The reader knows that the raising of Lazarus has provoked the Pharisees and the chief priests to take counsel to kill Jesus (11:53). This episode ends with a determination to kill Lazarus as well (vv. 10-11) "because on account of him many of the Jews were going away and believing in Jesus." The story of the woman is the focus of attention, but first the dire context of the story must be examined.

The preceding chapter (John 11) presents an extended account of the raising of Lazarus. The evangelist's literary skill is evident, emphasizing both Mary's faith in Jesus and her lack of understanding of who he really is. Jesus' declaration, "I am the resurrection and the life" (11:15) far exceeds her considerable faith. This powerful declaration also intensifies the determination of Jesus' opponents to put him to death. As soon as he has raised Lazarus, the threat which Jesus poses to existing authority structures is evident. "Many of the Jews . . . believed in him," causing the Pharisees, the council, the chief priests, and the high priest Caiaphas to take "counsel to put him to death" (11:45-53).

John identifies this opposition specifically in terms of the council's fear of Roman reprisals against messianic movements (9:48). These chief priests and Pharisees see themselves as doing the "expedient" thing (11:50), but they are ignorant of the consequences of their actions. In fact, they are not preserving the peace with Rome, because they are invoking God's wrath against Israel. Still in spite of themselves, they are preparing the way for the salvation that God has in mind for Israel. Jesus' death will be efficacious for both the nation of Judea and for the diaspora (11:52). But the Judean leaders have no grasp of what is truly happening.

John's comments about the "Jews" often sound anti-Jewish, and it is certainly difficult for modern gentile Christians to read these texts without reinforcing anti-Jewish sentiments. But the evangelist has differentiated the characters in the narrative. The Jewish people believe in Jesus. Their leaders in the council fear his popularity. These "Judeans" are the adversaries. The reader is also given insight to a deeper mystery. God is at work even through their opposition. Their blindness and ignorance are all the more ironic as they become more adamant, and their actions become transparently desperate.

As Passover approaches, the discrepancy increases between the faithful and the adversaries. The evangelist lets the reader glimpse the gathering storm. The people are going to Jerusalem to purify themselves, but the leaders are laying plans for a deed that would stain their hands with blood at the very time of the holy feast (11:55-57).

The episode with Mary in Bethany, therefore, is filled with meanings which the participants in the story only partially grasp. Perhaps Mary, Martha, Judas, Jesus, and the others know that the chief priests and Pharisees have ordered Jesus' arrest (11:55-57). Certainly the reader knows, and Jesus seems to understand. Jesus is the center of attention in the story, and Mary's loving care of Jesus fulfills her faith and thanksgiving at Lazarus' resurrection. The story does not stand alone, and there is nothing ordinary about this meal.

The synoptic gospels also tell of a woman anointing Jesus from "an alabaster flask of ointment" (Matt. 26:6-13; Mark 14:3-9; Luke 7:36-50). The similarities and differences of the accounts have long fascinated scholars. Whether or not these accounts remember the same event, the stories are significantly different.

Matthew tells the same story as Mark. Both Gospels locate the event in the house of Simon the Leper toward the end of Jesus' ministry. Some were offended at such extravagance in the face of the needs of the poor. But Jesus defended the woman's act as extraordinary. He would soon be gone, and she would be remembered for having prepared his body for burial.

Luke focuses upon the woman's reputation as a sinner. In Luke's account, Jesus is in the house of Simon the Pharisee, and Jesus' identity as a prophet is publicly tested by the encounter. Nothing is said in Luke about the poor, and the extravagance of the woman's act is only proof of the depth of her love at being forgiven and accepted.

The scene is more ominous in John. Only Judas objects to the extravagance of the woman's act, and the evangelist immediately identifies Judas as "the one who was to betray him" (12:4). Furthermore, John discredits Judas' objection about the poor and calls him a thief from the money box (12:6). These charges are the evangelist's emphases. Jesus' rejoinder to Judas is thus even sharper. Both Judas and Mary are preparing for Jesus' burial, but their motives, knowledge, and actions are completely different.

The traditional word about the perpetual presence of the poor (11:9; see also Matt. 26:11 and Mark 14:7) is not cynical. Nor is it an easy justification for lavish expenditures by the disciples of Jesus. In all three Gospels (Matthew, Mark, John), it is Jesus' defense of the woman's generous act in the face of criticism, and all these accounts link this anointing with Jesus' burial. Perhaps these Gospels also convey a historical reminiscence about the women who came to anoint Jesus on Easter. Certainly all three see this as a foreshadowing of Jesus' death.

John drives the point home at the close of the episode. The positive response of the "great crowd of the Jews" now provokes the chief priests to plot Lazarus' death as well. It is not enough to plot to kill the one who is "the resurrection and the life." They are now also compelled to kill the one who was raised to life.

John is not promoting an anti-Jewish prejudice, although many modern interpreters have twisted the story in that direction. John is depicting a very positive reception among the Jewish or Judean people. But the religious leaders who are in league with the Romans have become adamant. John's analysis takes the reader deep into the conflict with power structures.

Proclamation: Jesus' death was not mere caprice or violence. This is not simply a story of prejudice or even of good people versus bad people. The mounting tide of violence in John's narrative swells from the depths of human rejection of Jesus' reign, even of him as "the resurrection and the life." The prejudices of Judeans versus Galileans and chief priests versus Jews are symbols and symptoms of profound vested interests. Judas' plea for the needs of the poor appears to be thinly veiled greed, but much more is at stake in Jesus' death than that.

As a morality lesson, John's story reveals the truth about the motives of the characters. It is a great story on that level, reminding the reader that things are often not as they seem and people may have dire ulterior motives. John directly reveals the schemes to kill Jesus and Lazarus, and Judas' hypocrisy. Those who think that the Fourth Gospel is more "spiritual" may be shocked at its candor and cold analysis. Similarly those who think that Christian preaching should avoid unpleasant moral judgments will need to repress much of this story. Faithful interpretation and proclamation of John's gospel lead directly into the world of conflicting interests and perverted moralities. John's account may be too much for the morally naive to take.

John's literary art also deserves more than admiration. It should be emulated in preaching. The tale to be told is not a morality fable. It is a true story filled with tragedy. Seeking to keep the peace and preserve their lives, Jesus' adversaries plan to kill the one who gives life, and even the one who was restored to life, Lazarus. This is more than good people opposed by bad. This is a struggle of love and justice with forces of chaos and destruction. The characters in the story are caught up in a drama which reaches beyond each episode. The deeper currents flow through this stretch of the story, and they surface only in brief exchanges between Mary and Jesus or Judas and Jesus.

The gospel truth is not a mere fact or announcement. It is a revelation which touches life in an enduring and dynamic way. This is one of the reasons for exploring the longer story of Holy Week slowly and persistently. The preacher is the teller, pulling the hearer into the complex relationships where Jesus is loved, even by those who were recently disappointed. But Jesus is also mistrusted, and finally betrayed by others who have experienced the same dramatic event of the raising of Lazarus.

As the story develops throughout Holy Week, it reveals the tragic blindness of humanity to the source of their salvation. The adversaries emerge clearly, but even Mary and the disciples have only a vague notion of the story that is unfolding around them. The evangelist invites the faithful of every age inside this process of disclosure, and the proclaimer does well to bring the hearers patiently along at each stage of the story.

The evangelist's confidence, of course, is deeper than literary art, pressing beyond morality or tragedy. As the narrative develops with its painful encounters and its revelations of deceit, faith, betrayal, and plots, God continues to be at work. Jesus is not marching blindly, ignorantly to his death. He is moving obediently, purposefully toward the strange glorification of the Son of man that lies ahead at the cross, and this is God's way of salvation (see 3:14-16; 12:23; 13:31).

Proclamation in Holy Week is revelation, filled with confidence of God's grace and salvation. But this confidence is not escapist or trivial. The realities of human immorality and blindness must be faced, because they are disclosed in the story. These realities are thus the context within which the greater mystery of God's salvation in Christ Jesus is also revealed. The truth about humanity and the gospel truth are met in the story of Holy Week.

Tuesday in Holy Week

Lutheran	Roman Catholic	Episcopal	Common Lectionary
Isa. 49:1-6	Isa. 49:1-6	Isa. 49:1-6	Isa. 49:1-7
1 Cor. 1:18-25		1 Cor. 1:18-31	1 Cor. 1:18-31
John 12:20-36	John 13:21-33, 36-38	John 12:37-50 *or* 42-50 *or* Mark 11:15-19	John 12:20-36

Collect for Tuesday in Holy Week: Lord Jesus, you have called us to follow you. Grant that our love may not grow cold in your service, and that we may not fail or deny you in the hour of trial. Amen.

FIRST LESSON: ISAIAH 49:1-6

Text: The second song of the servant in Isaiah 40–55 is one of the great "call" texts of the Bible. As in Exodus 3, 1 Samuel 3, Isaiah 6, or Jeremiah

1, where God called a leader or prophet, the song includes a dialogue with God. The servant who speaks in the first person in vv. 1-2 and 4-5 is identified by God in v. 3 as "Israel, in whom I will be glorified." In v. 6, God announces the full impact of the commission.

Verse 1 is a text to memorize. It is filled with a profound sense of God's secret and complex ways of working through human agents. The prophet speaks of himself as called from his mother's womb, named from within her body. This is a declaration to the coastlands, to the world. As in Jeremiah (1:5) and Paul (Gal. 1:15), the mystery of divine election and call resists all simplistic solutions. On the lips of the faithful, however, these are words of assurance of God's prior decision.

Verse 2 is a testimony to the role of the chosen one as an implement in God's peculiar artillery. The prophet never imagines that God's call is a personal privilege or status. This call is a means for God to accomplish God's purposes, an implement of warfare, like a sharp sword or polished arrow. The servant himself is God's secret weapon, hidden away for the critical time. In v. 3, therefore, God speaks directly about the call of the servant as Israel, "in whom I will be glorified."

Some scholars have argued that the link with "Israel" is an editorial gloss, an attempt by the author to move beyond personalistic callings to Israel's election. The line between person and corporate personality in the Old Testament is blurred in any case. The identity of the "Servant" is a fascinating historical problem, but God's purpose in this call is the more significant issue. In the larger context of Isaiah 40–55, God's reputation has been at stake, especially as "Lord," "God," and "Savior." The contest with the gods of the nations has been fiercely contested, and Israel's fate has been crucial to God's honor (see especially Isa. 43:3-13; 45:15-17).

God's glorification (Isa. 49:3) is hidden in Israel's vindication. Israel is not only a secret weapon, but in this servant, the secret of the world is hidden and revealed. The God who chooses and calls such an unlikely people is not about to ignore them. Israel is instrumental to the vindication and glorification of God as Lord and Savior of the world.

Verses 5-6, therefore, move directly into God's mission in this servant, Israel. All along, from being formed in the womb, the servant's role has been honored and fortified with the strength of God. The first purpose has been the restoration of Israel. The gathering and return of the people in exile is the work of God, exercised through human agents. But God has had more in mind since the call in the womb, and before. God has intended to rule and be acknowledged in the whole world, and God's glorious plan and call for restored Israel is now revealed.

The great themes of the *missio Dei* sound forcefully in these chapters of Isaiah (see also 52:10). Verse 6 again underscores the restoration of

Israel from exile as God's salvation, but restoration does not exhaust God's saving activity. The restoration of Israel proves to be the restoration of the call of the servant to be a light to the nations. Israel's glory is the reflection of God's splendid saving reign. God's determined will from before the birth of the servant has been salvation to the end of the earth (see also 52:10).

Proclamation: Ascension Day and Pentecost follow Holy Week, and the mission texts of Acts 1–2 announce the call of Jesus' followers to be his witnesses. The commission of Isaiah 49:6 is echoed in the question and answer between Jesus and his followers. Mere restoration of Israel will not suffice. Witness to his reign and salvation are to reach "unto the end of the earth" (Acts 1:6-8).

Christians may fear that such affirmations sound like a new triumphalism or religious imperialism. Once Constantine had identified the cross as the sign by which to conquer, history has had ample brutality and oppression wrought in Jesus' name.

Isaiah, however, had little reason to fear triumphalism. The issue was survival of the faithful in the midst of foreign deities. The triumph appeared to belong to the neo-Babylonian empire and to the Persians. Israel was no threat. So also those Christians who yearn for God to be vindicated while they endure humiliation or persecution are not triumphalists. Biblical faith and even the Lord's prayer instruct the faithful always to look and pray for the coming of the kingdom on earth and unto the ends of the earth.

The more difficult question, however, is whether God's reign will be sought and welcomed on earth. The prophet is full of confidence that God has begun to do a new thing which will result in the restoration of the servant Israel to her call. This people has been redeemed for the sake of the mission which God still intends to pursue. So what happens when God begins to act? The conviction that God means business may be as awesome as the fear that God had forgotten Israel was frightening.

God does not call people for the sake of making them important. Those who follow Jesus' call to discipleship are not assured of clout, success, or great reputations. God rules through human servants, not through coercive power or conquering heroes. Israel in exile had again learned the lesson of God's hidden strength, and the call of the servant was a token of God's peculiar triumph. Both those who suffer and those who are enjoying great success need to hear this unusual word of God's saving ways.

Those who suffer must understand that the prophet does not glorify weakness for its own sake. There is no moral or psychological virtue in suffering. Even v. 7 (see the Common Lectionary) expresses no pleasure in the fact that the nations despised and abhorred the servant. All of this is but a setting for showing forth the "strength" of God in the midst of human weakness (see also v. 5b).

The glorification of suffering may only double the misery of the afflicted, especially if it is used as an official theology. Pastors who counsel victims of family violence to endure abuse as from God may only justify the abuser. The hope for those who suffer the "slings and arrows of outrageous fortune" rather lies in the assurance of God's greater will to vindicate and save the oppressed. And through them, God intends to save the world. Even their sufferings will be redeemed, because the world is full of oppression which they recognize as idolatry.

Christian preaching of the cross is a mighty protest against self-satisfied religions of success. The high and mighty are brought low from their thrones. So also Holy Week is a reminder to the faithful that the death of Jesus is not a benediction on the life-styles of the rich and famous. But neither does his death glorify misery. All along, the saving reign of God is being revealed in a most surprising way, equipping faithful witnesses to God's righteous reign in a world of conflicting claims. God's strength and faithfulness are shown forth in the human weakness of the servant, particularly the Servant Messiah Jesus.

EPISTLE: 1 CORINTHIANS 1:18-25

Text: The first four chapters of 1 Corinthians expound Christian wisdom. Paul has entered the world of the teachers of wisdom, and he is able to speak their language. But Paul resists the teachers of his age. The gospel he proclaims is not merely another plausible philosophy because God's ways are not subject to human sensibility.

The opening and closing verses of this reading must interpret each other. Paul is not merely glorifying foolishness. Nor is he insisting that the gospel must be believed because it makes no sense. Instead, the apostle is commending the divine wisdom of the cross. The "folly" of the cross (v. 18) and "the foolishness of God" (v. 25) are only foolish according to the worldly standards of "the wisdom of the wise" and the "cleverness of the clever" (v. 19; Isaiah 29:14). The cross is God's strategy to confound those who insist that their standards of wisdom and power are ultimate.

Interpreters have struggled to understand why Paul would press such an unusual argument. The larger context indicates a competitive spirit between followers of Paul, Apollos, Cephas, and perhaps even Christ (see 1:12, 3:4, 22). Loyalty to teachers in the faith had become party spirit. The Hellenistic world was full of such examples of partisan loyalties to Socrates, Diogenes, or Epicurus, and the Christians were tempted to regard their teachers in the same manner.

In the complex religious culture of Corinth, superior "wisdom" and "power" were often claimed in the name of a master teacher. The followers of Jesus confronted a marketplace of philosophy, cultic observance, oriental wisdom, and traditional Greek practices. Gurus, mystagogues, mediums, and priests vied for the loyalties and souls of the believers. As the rest of Paul's correspondence with the Corinthians indicates, the Christians were quickly enmeshed in issues of spiritual wisdom, food laws, charismatic teachers, inspired speech, and holy writings. The danger of division among the Christians was intensified by the competitive religious climate of the Hellenistic city.

Paul's argument, therefore, cut through all of this posturing about superior teachers, wisdom, and power. Christians were not to become enmeshed in petty loyalties and partisan claims. When contention for advantage characterized the wisdom of the age, a faith oriented to service seemed naive and foolish. Paul saw that such foolishness was really God's wisdom, and in such folly the Christians were united with the saving word they proclaimed from God.

Proclamation: Holy Week is a critical opportunity to grasp the power and wisdom of the "theology of the cross" in a context of pluralism. The vision of "Christ and culture" is quite remarkable. Jesus is not another guru or avatar of salvation, and his disciples are not set in competition with each other to "market" this religion with greater displays of power or more impressive wisdom. The mission of the gospel takes its cue from God's peculiar wisdom and power, resisting the ways of the world.

If this text is not preached because so few congregations hold worship services on Tuesday of Holy Week, its powerful witness must be offered in other settings. Any congregation which intends to proclaim a public word of salvation must come to terms with this radical assessment of the religious marketplace. The "theology of the cross" is not a withdrawal into a secret piety. The cross reveals a divine strategy which unites public witness, declaring a wisdom and salvation which could only come from God.

Modern programs of evangelism often grow impatient with theological niceties, finding much academic "wisdom" to be irrelevant. Paul also refused to be drawn into a dispute about the wisdom of Apollos or Cephas. The "wisdom of the wise" and the "cleverness of the clever" may only produce party spirit.

At the same time, Christians can not merely adopt the methods of the world on the grounds that they are more effective. If Jesus were merely a product to be marketed, the issue would be that of his distinctive appeal or "market niche." And the television evangelists and Christian bookshops know well that the Christian gospel must make its way in a public marketplace of ideas and claims. But then how shall we proceed?

Paul says, "We preach Christ crucified, a stumbling block to Jews and a folly to Gentiles." Certainly the apostle is not withdrawing from the public arena. Neither will he package Jesus in the form of the powerful "sign" or "eloquent wisdom" sought by various segments of the population, "lest the cross of Christ be emptied of its power" (1:17).

Holy Week is a discipline for the Christian congregation to learn the ways of God. The benefit of the gospel takes the form of deepest human need. It is patient, attentive to sin and suffering, and wrought of love. Those who are tempted to rush to the glory of Easter and the displays of Pentecost must first learn the "theology of the cross." This is not an academic nicety. It is the revelation of the power and wisdom of God.

Much more than a practice of personal penance, the proclamation of Christ crucified is God's word of hope. This gospel defines the distinctive direction of Christian mission in the public marketplace. Even more importantly, it reveals the depth and strength of the salvation and hope which God offers the world and us in Christ Jesus.

GOSPEL: JOHN 12:20-36

Text: The Gospel for Monday (John 12:1-11) was filled with morality lessons, tied into larger ironies of the growing tragedy of rejection of Jesus. The triumphal entry (John 12:12-19) follows, emphasizing the disciples' lack of understanding and the growing aversion of the Pharisees to the crowds. The scene is ominous, and Jesus' popularity foreshadows his death. The meaning of all of this in God's plan will only be clear on the other side of Jesus' "glorification" (12:16).

The appearance of the "Greeks" in 12:20 is complete with a formal request to Philip, who gathers Andrew to present their petition to Jesus. It is not clear whether these "Greeks" were Gentiles or Hellenistic Jews. They were in the group going to Jerusalem for the feast, but they were not "Judean" Jews. Their arrival is a significant occasion.

In 7:35, the "Jews" had already wondered whether Jesus intended "to go to the Dispersion among the Greeks and teach the Greeks." Those were the Pharisees' concerns, lest Jesus gain popularity among people beyond their influence. Thus John provides a glimpse into the complex power relationships in Israel. The appearance of the "Greeks" then amplifies the Pharisees' fears that "the world has gone after him" (12:19). For Jesus this signals the arrival of the hour of the glorification of the Son of man (12:23). The politics and theology are tied closely together.

The evangelist emphasizes that Jesus understands this as the encounter of God's mission with opposing human and suprahuman forces. The "hour" of glorification (v. 23) is the "hour" for which Jesus has come (v. 27). This "hour" cannot be avoided (v. 27). This is the moment of "the judgment of this world, now shall the ruler of this world be cast out" (v. 31).

The glorification of Jesus is also explicated. This "lifting up" of the Son of man is not an ordinary exaltation. It is a genuine enthronement whereby the exalted ruler may draw up his faithful with him into safety and dominion (v. 32), but it is an exaltation by means of being lifted up in death. Jesus' words about his being "lifted up from the earth" are followed immediately by the comment of the evangelist: "He said this to show by what death he was to die" (v. 33).

Jesus is the major interpreter in the story. He sees his death coming because he recognizes the political reality of his adversaries. He also presents this as a cosmic struggle with the ruler of this world because more than flesh and blood are contending here. Above all, he testifies that this is not merely God's judgment descending on the world, but God's salvation at work in the Son of man.

The entire episode could be interpreted as an elaboration of John 3:16-17. Both God's judgment and love for the world are at work. This is God's will to save, and faith in this Son of man is trust in God. The way of salvation will involve dying.

Verses 24-26 and 35-36, therefore, are counsels on faith and discipleship. These are traditional words that also make sense outside of the context of this encounter. Like interludes in the narrative, they bring the reader deeper into the heart of what all of this means for the faithful. These are classic Lenten themes, revealing the cost and promise of faithful discipleship.

Proclamation: The preacher must make a decision. Will this be a sermon about the encounter between Jesus and the ruler(s) of this world, or will this be a meditation on discipleship? The text is rich in possibilities for both sermons, but the preacher would need the art of the fourth evangelist to handle both dimensions in one sermon. Perhaps the dramatic truth of the encounter will fit better in a public setting, and the reflections on discipleship would be more appropriate in a small gathering of the faithful.

Jesus' encounter with the powers also has great spiritual depth. His own sense of gravity pervades the story, especially when he declares, "Now is my soul troubled" (v. 27). The only passion that the adversaries feel is apparently blind rage, but the Messiah is caught up in the love of God (3:16) so that his anguish is not so much at his own fate but for his disciples and even his adversaries.

What we see through Jesus' insight, however, is the reality of conflicting wills and reigns. The arrival of the Greeks is not a cause for celebration. Jesus knows that the adversaries will regard this as reason to put their murder plot in motion.

An experienced pastor once said that we should quit being anxious about why more outsiders are not joining the church. We would see the matter more clearly if we admitted that newcomers threaten us. Then we would see how our vested interests regularly keep strangers away. This is not mere cynicism, but it tells a truth that we fear. Just so, the Gospel story explores why and how the arrival of the Greeks signaled an escalating threat to Jesus from the religious leaders.

More is happening than mere politics. A larger struggle is occurring in the narrative and in this world. The chief priests and Pharisees may think they are being clever in cutting this popular preacher down to size and eliminating him. But even they are not in control of "why" they are so opposed.

Jesus reveals that beneath the morality lesson, behind the political screen, the drama has cosmic proportions. The ancient readers had a much more lively sense of being caught in a struggle with principalities and powers. Whether contending with the fates and fortunes of Greece or Rome or the spiritual powers of Persia, they knew they lived in the presence of forces that were beyond them. Their rulers reinforced this larger view with their constant claims to divine authority.

The modern world often minimizes such religious claims. Life itself is reduced in scope. "That's just politics," people say. Or "It's all a matter of economic interests or psychological needs." Even Christians are tempted to reduce salvation to merely personal terms as if there were no larger realities than the self.

This story, however, leads the faithful into a larger realm. The politics and self-interest are real. But in the midst of these mundane factors, God is contending to save the world through Christ Jesus. It is Jesus who keeps pulling back the curtain to reveal the magnitude of the struggle and the plight of the human beings who are involved far beyond their comprehension.

Jesus' gravity is also matched by his clarity. The first lesson is that this is going to be a hard struggle, and the second message is that God intends to triumph in salvation. Dire as the conflict may become, the message of Holy Week is not finally gloomy. The powers of evil are real, but not ultimate. Jesus is unswerving in his purpose, and his vision of his exaltation in crucifixion is filled with hope for those whom he will draw to himself. The plane of politics and involvement with forces and powers will not finally capture those who look to the Son of man lifted up (see also John 3:14).

The sermon on discipleship, therefore, is also a word of reassurance. The voice from heaven verifies Jesus' vision (v. 28), encouraging his followers to listen to his words of counsel about following in his way. Jesus does not go blindly or tragically to death. His path draws his followers beyond death to life and light.

Those who follow Jesus see the world and their lives in a new light. The struggles of this world are more than political, although human interests are in mighty conflict. Life involves more than moral choices, especially since people are so often blind to what is good and true. The coming of Jesus, the "light of the world" (8:12), reveals the world in a new light.

The path of Holy Week is an illumined walk. The darkness is revealed in its depth, and the power of sin is fully recognized. But all the way, Jesus *is* the light, leading *to* the light. The glory that lies ahead is all the more splendid because of Jesus' conquest of humiliation and darkness.

Wednesday in Holy Week

Lutheran	Roman Catholic	Episcopal	Common Lectionary
Isa. 50:4-9a	Isa. 50:4-9	Isa. 50:4-9a	Isa. 50:4-9a
Rom. 5:6-11		Heb. 9:11-15, 24-28	Heb. 12:1-3
Matt. 26:14-25	Matt. 26:14-25	John 13:21-35 *or* Matt. 26:1-5, 14-25	John 13:21-30

Collect for Wednesday in Holy Week: Almighty God, your Son our Savior suffered at the hands of men and women and endured the shame of the cross. Grant that we may walk in the way of his cross and find in the way of life and peace; through your Son, Jesus Christ our Lord. Amen.

FIRST LESSON: ISAIAH 50:4-9a

Text: This text is identical to the reading for the Sunday of the Passion at the beginning of Holy Week. Everything that was said in that context about this servant song still applies, but now the Gospel texts (Matt. 26:14-25 and John 13:21-30) highlight Jesus' encounters with the betrayer, Judas. The last verses in the passage from Isaiah stand out, as if Jesus had spoken them: "Who will contend with me? Let us stand up together. Who is my adversary? Let him come near to me. Behold, the Lord God helps me; who will declare me guilty?"

Proclamation: The Bible is never surprised at the appearance of an adversary or accuser. The servant who suffers is not inflicting pain upon himself or seeking salvation through his dishonor. Nor is Holy Week a ritual of self-denigration. The Scriptures continue to focus upon the struggle between God's holy will and human willfulness. No masochism is allowed, but realism requires that the servants of God know what and whom they are up against.

The latter verses of this servant song are an excellent source for again grasping the severe diagnosis and deep hope of the biblical vision. False accusations, character assassination, and even physical violence may be expected, but never welcomed. They may be expected because God's faithful servants will expose idolatries, false salvations, and deceitful pieties. Those who are witnesses to God's justice and mercy will provoke reactions from people and systems which claim divine sanctification for their vested interests. The servant will not be able to prevent conflict and may well be at its center.

Hope, however, persists at a deeper level, grounded in God's promises. This confidence in God assures the faithful even in the midst of angry attacks and betrayals, perhaps especially then. Bitter recriminations are not pleasant, but they are not unexpected either. Nor do they dislodge the faithful from their sense of security or hope. On the contrary, the servants of God can see that an irrational, hostile world has been exposed in the sure light of the word of God.

Faith in God is tested in these circumstances. Unswerving trust in God's promises will be difficult to sustain. But the texts of Holy Week offer more than an appeal to human persistence. They reveal God's determined will to triumph in love and justice in the face of real adversaries.

EPISTLE: ROMANS 5:6-11

Text: In this text, Paul articulates one of the most radical and shocking themes of Christian proclamation, the justification of the ungodly. This is Paul's testimony to "God's love for us" (5:6, 8). No usual theory of religious progress or moral improvement can tolerate the idea that Christ died for the ungodly, for sinners, and even for the enemies of God. But Paul insists on God's justification, salvation, and reconciliation for exactly these. The holiness of God's righteousness is at stake, fulfilled in love. Paul will tolerate no compromise.

In Paul's world, these words stunned both the Jews and the Greeks. Those who knew the Scriptures of Israel observed God's laws in order to be godly, to avoid being sinners, and to be friends of God. What else would proper religious people do?

They also relied on God's mercy to compensate for their deficiencies in keeping the law. But why confess more sin than you have committed, and why would anyone suggest that God's salvation was intended specifically for the ungodly?

Paul's gospel also offended the moral universe of the Greeks and Romans. In time it would assault the medieval system of penance for sins. Rituals of purification, penance, and absolution have long been remedies offered to the penitent. A declaration of God's love for the ungodly, sinners, and enemies seems to wreak havoc on orderly religion. It is not hard to see why Paul's letter was such a threat to the Pharisees of his age and to church authorities of later eras.

The death of Jesus is God's deed, wrought through the hands of sinful humanity, but for the sake of sinners. In Paul's testimony, the blood of Christ justifies (v. 9), but not only through satisfaction for sin, as if Christ's blood could supplement godly penance. Rather, in Jesus' death, God took on the world of sin, including the perpetrators of Jesus' death and the rest of us who are complicit in sin. God's love is an active force in the world, not merely a compensation for failures.

As Paul continues the argument in Romans 5, it is clear that Jesus' death is a divine encounter with the power or dominion of sin. Whether humans are more or less righteous is not the issue because God is not supplementing the inadequacy of human penance. Sin is a power in the world, and death its common result. The faithful are thus the first to discover their bondage to sin, their alienation and hostility to God. They dare to admit this reality because they now know its remedy, wrought by God.

Proclamation: "Wretched man that I am!" says Paul in Romans 7:24. "Who will deliver me from this body of death?"

The assertion does not demean humanity, and the question has an answer. The gospel of Jesus Christ is the declaration of God's deliverance "while we were yet sinners."

The logic, however, attacks usual religious reasoning. As long as the question is, "What must I do to inherit eternal life?", Paul's counsel, like Jesus', will be unrelenting. "If it is up to you, you must do everything.

Anything less than perfection will fall short of the holy righteousness of God. Frankly, your religious efforts will only reveal your animosity to God because you will not be able to make it right."

Love is the only human analogy that comes close to grasping the peculiar logic of God's mercy. Here assertions of "merit" and "worthiness" fail again, while the ardor of the lover for the beloved inspires dramatic initiatives. The love stories of the world are full of accounts of dramatic rescues and immense sacrifice for the sake of the beloved. Never will the lover ponder whether the beloved is "worth it."

If we deal with Holy Week as a ritual of penance, striving to qualify for God's forgiveness, even to close the gap so that God's mercy can reach us, we miss the point. Paul's logic in Romans 5 will then only confound us again in our efforts to prove our worth.

Holy Week is an excellent time for love stories. That is what this whole revelation of God's holy righteousness turns out to be. The logic of love does not count cost, does not demean, does not humiliate the enemy, and does not condemn.

A small boy had irritated his mother most of one rainy afternoon, finally putting a gouge in her prized table in an act of defiance. She sent him to his room to ponder his sins while she cooled off and considered what to do with him. He then peered around the corner before he was welcome. He wore a sad face, realizing his error. He reached out to her with the words, "I'm sorry. Don't be angry. We've got to keep the loving going."

Pascal affirmed that "The heart has reasons which reason knows nothing of." Paul's argument in Romans is full of reasons, but they arise from the reason of the heart of God, altering the logic of mere moral discourse. Human lovers may understand better than those who must tend the structures of law and order. God's venture in Jesus is born of a passion to forgive, to reconcile, to save sinful humanity.

People who are sensible and reasonable may be offended at such displays of love, even by God. They may regard the preoccupation with the lost as unworthy or unwise priorities, especially for God. But for those who know their need of God's love and forgiveness, this testimony to God's radical commitment to love us deals realistically with the principalities and powers to which we are so often subject and gives us reason to rejoice, far beyond the hope which conventional religious reason supplies.

GOSPEL: MATTHEW 26:14-25

Text: The story of the betrayal, arrest, trial, and death of Jesus requires all the art and conviction of every narrator. The four evangelists of the New Testament and the modern teller of the tale share the task of conveying this most awesome drama in human history in the economy of a few scenes.

Matthew begins this climax of his story of Jesus in 26:1 by marking the conclusion of Jesus' teaching on the Mount of Olives (24:3—25:46) and announcing the impending betrayal. Following Mark's sequence straight through to Jesus' burial (27:61), Matthew's version preserves the rhythm of Mark's story and offers elaborations rather than corrections.

Mark's sequence had already revealed the complexity of this story by brief episodes which introduced the hostile intentions of the chief priests and scribes, coupled with their fear of the people (Mark 14:1-2). Matthew (26:3-5) elaborated the list of the adversaries by locating the evil collusion in the palace of the high priest Caiaphas in a deliberative discussion with the elders of the people. Both Mark (14:3-9) and Matthew (26:6-13) then change the scene to Jesus in Bethany where a faithful woman anoints him with costly ointment, and the secret embassy of Judas to the chief priests brings these scenes together in his betrayal. The story has many actors. The question is, whose will shall be accomplished?

The question is sharpened in Matthew's account in which Judas asks the chief priests, "What are you willing to give me if I deliver him to you?" Judas has taken an initiative which fits with the covert counsel of the high priests "to arrest Jesus by stealth and kill him" (26:4). We are not told how Judas learned of the intentions of the chief priests, but we recognize a faithless and greedy act as surely as we have just seen the faithful and generous act of the woman who anointed Jesus. Judas has "bought in" on the conspiracy to kill Jesus. From now on, he is committed to seeking an "opportunity" for betrayal. His price of thirty pieces of silver was probably about four months wages for a day laborer.

The scene moves back to Jesus once more, where he is preparing for the Passover. Jesus' arrangements soon reveal that he is staging the scene with great insight. The high priests may think they are manipulating the events. The woman who anoints Jesus may only understand partially the great significance which Jesus assigns to her act. Judas may think he is in control, and all of these agents are disclosing their wills in their deeds. But the reader and Jesus can see that all of these people are caught up in a story far beyond their understanding.

Jesus' word about his impending betrayal is an oracle, disrupting the order of the Passover ritual with the truth of what is really happening in the story, or about to happen. "One of you will betray me!" For all those who do not know what Judas has been doing, this word is an occasion for sorrowful self-examination. They ask, one after another, "Is it I, Lord?" (v. 22), until it narrows down to "the one who has dipped his hand in the dish with me" (v. 23).

Jesus' next word is about himself and that betrayer. It is an exceptionally complex oracle, going far beyond prediction to a revelation of how the death of the Son of man is the fulfillment of the will of God and the act of betrayal is the defiance of God's will. God's salvation will be accomplished through the fate of the Son of man, but God's judgment will fall upon the one whose complicity with the forces of evil leads to betrayal. Now the matters of "will" and "culpability" are sharply stated. This is not a theoretical discussion. This is a narrative disclosure of what is happening in the presence of God and these witnesses. This is a final and severe warning to Judas, if he has the ears to hear it. It is also a revelation to the reader of how God's saving purpose could be at work in the midst of the intrigue of evildoers.

Judas' only response is a cooler form of the disciples' earlier question, "Is it I, master?" There is no hint of remorse, and even the title could be used of any rabbi or teacher (see 8:19 and Judas again at 26:49). His question might be rendered, "Is that my fate you are pronouncing, teacher?" And Jesus' answer is, "You said it."

The conversation is cryptic to those who do not know all that has happened. But Jesus clearly knows as a prophet. Judas should understand since he knows what he has said to the high priests. The reader clearly knows that this brief exchange is freighted with meaning, revealing Jesus' fate, God's will, and the real but limited power of evil.

Matthew's version of the betrayal indicates very little about Judas' final motive, and modern novelists have been unwilling to let it rest. Furthermore, nothing is said about how Judas felt or to what extent Jesus himself knew all of the details of Judas' visit to the high priests. Jesus' words are pronouncements. Perhaps they are meant as prophetic declarations in which the speaker himself only partially grasps their significance. Neither Matthew nor Mark insists that Jesus had an omniscient understanding of Judas' actions.

But neither was Jesus naive or ignorant. God had seen Judas initiate this betrayal, and the reader was privy to the scene. Jesus' pronouncements were at least revelations of the truth of what was happening and about to happen. Jesus had seen what was coming. His disciples were alerted, and Judas had been warned. The God of Israel does not trick humans into tragic errors where they blindly go to their fate while intending the best.

The matter remains complex, because of the way it is with the human will. The truth had been disclosed to Judas and the other disciples, but had they been able to hear and see?

Proclamation: God knows the way it is with us. The world is not so simple as to be divided into "good people" and "bad people." None of us is able of living in full conformity with God's will, but there are differing kinds of complicity with the forces of evil. The faithfulness of the woman who squandered the ointment on Jesus, the ignorance of the eleven, and the active betrayal of Judas are not the same.

We watch Judas in horror. He is one of the twelve closest to Jesus, surreptitiously approaching those who are committed to kill his Lord and Master. He makes a deal for a paltry sum and returns to the intimacy of the Lord's Passover table. This is betrayal at its worst, continuing to feign fidelity.

Modern interpreters are fascinated with Judas' motives. Books like *The Passover Plot* or *Judas, My Brother,* and the musical "Jesus Christ Superstar" are filled with speculation about why Judas betrayed Jesus. Was he trying to force Jesus' hand, hoping to galvanize popular resistance to Roman rule? Had he lost hope in Jesus' program of nonviolent resistance? Did he expect God to intervene if the Messiah was actually threatened with death? Modern interpreters are generally compelled to find a psychological explanation for Judas' actions, and preachers are often drawn into such speculation.

The ancient art of the narrator requires greater integrity of the preacher. Judas' betrayal is not easily explained. As actor and as pawn, Judas "struts and frets his hour upon the stage and then is heard no more" (to use Shakespeare's words). The story rivets our attention on his perversity and his plight, drawing us deeper into the mystery of human complicity with the forces of evil. If Judas were purely evil, perhaps we could dismiss him, distance him from ourselves. If he were simply misguided, we could forgive him, as we would also wish to excuse ourselves.

How shall we understand Jesus' indirect words about himself and Judas, "that man by whom the Son of man is betrayed"? The passive voice implies an actor, and Judas is the betrayer. But is Judas the real actor? Surely he is warned and held accountable for his action. And if "the Son of man goes as it is written of him," how shall this passive voice be understood? Who is directing the script for the Son of man?

The evangelist has woven Jesus' complex oracles into the narrative in such a way as to resist easy answers. Like the Hebrew prophets and the Greek tragic poets, Matthew has told the tale of betrayal without letting the betrayer or the reader escape. The horror and the fascination are compounded by watching the betrayer make his moves, cut his devious deals, and hear the Master's warnings and judgments.

But Judas will not actually hear, until it is too late. After he has hailed Jesus as "Master," greeted him with a kiss, and been welcomed by Jesus as "Friend" in the act of betrayal (26:49-50), Judas will approach the chief priests and the elders, confessing his sin of betraying innocent blood (27:3-10). But he will find no forgiveness there, only condemnation.

The story of Judas deserves greater attention in the context of Holy Week because of its compelling depth. This is a story of political intrigue with the pro-Roman high priests desperately struggling to "keep the peace" and save their positions. It is a story of the Messiah's peculiar program of dominion through humiliation, even death on the cross. It is a story of hope and despair of all those people and followers who surround the Messiah on his way to the cross. And it is also a story of human compromise, complicity, and betrayal, driving the reader to see one whom Jesus calls "Friend" revealed as betrayer.

Jesus' reign reveals God's saving purpose. The larger story is an insistent witness that the principalities and powers with all of their forces of death were not able to prevail against the dominion of this merciful Messiah. But the bright light of this revelation also discloses the depth of human sin.

Before the awful act of betrayal is completed, Jesus discerns the foul deed and reveals its consequences for him and the betrayer. The other disciples are confused, and the betrayer does not see. But from the far side of Easter, the Christian believer watches in horror and wonders with each of the disciples in turn, "Is it I, Lord?"

Maundy Thursday

Lutheran	Roman Catholic	Episcopal	Common Lectionary
Exod. 12:1-14	Exod. 12:1-8, 11-14	Exod. 12:1-14a	Exod. 12:1-14
1 Cor. 11:17-32	1 Cor. 11:23-26	1 Cor. 11:23-26	1 Cor. 11:23-26
John 13:1-17, 34	John 13:1-15	John 13:1-15	John 13:1-15

Collect for Maundy Thursday: Holy God, source of all love, on the night of his betrayal, Jesus gave his disciples a new commandment: To love one another as he had loved them. By your Holy Spirit write this commandment in our hearts; through your Son, Jesus Christ our Lord, who lives and reigns with you and the Holy Spirit, one God, now and forever. Amen.

FIRST LESSON: EXODUS 12:1-14

Text: The Passover story is foundational for Israel. This was the turning point in the exodus from slavery in Egypt. Verses 2-14 are all direct commands from God, spoken to Moses and overheard by countless generations in Israel and the Christian church. All of the details are carefully prescribed, the month, the day, the hours, the unblemished year-old male lamb, the unleavened bread and bitter herbs, the manner of cooking, the manner of eating, the disposition of the leftovers, down to the blood on the two doorposts and the lintel of the houses. Everything is ordered, marking "the whole assembly of the congregation of Israel" for salvation in the midst of a nation marked for judgment.

Anthropologists will recognize the significance of such attention to detail. Many religions of the world are equally meticulous about their rituals, often intended to control divine forces with sympathetic magic. The spell or incantation must be performed exactly right to achieve the desired effect. All rites and liturgies tend to be preoccupied with specifics and forms.

The specifics in the Passover story, however, are focused on human obedience, not on influencing God. God is the one who is setting Israel apart. The symbols of the ritual seek to influence and identify this distinctive people, drawing the experience of the flight from Egypt into the details of the meal. This is a feast for a people preparing to move out, already clothed for travel, staff in hand, eating in haste, not leaving a trace in the morning. God is the teacher, and the details of the ritual are all part of the lesson which Israel must learn.

The ritual does not itself produce Israel's salvation, as if any people could merely replicate the magic. Israel is being instructed in God's ordering of the world, and this God is the source of hope and freedom for the enslaved.

It would be fascinating to know more about the meal practices that appear to be contrasted by these commands. This is an unusual meal in any culture. The blood of the lamb is not offered as a sacrifice to God, but it is "a sign for you" which God also promises to observe. And the meal is emphatically communal, bringing small households together. No one eats this feast alone, and nothing is left behind. The practices are full of lessons, large and small. Above all, this is a meal ritual established by God for the salvation of the people.

Proclamation: "Why is this night different from all other nights?" asks the youngest member of the household on Passover evening. The story and the practices are woven together to teach and identify the youngest and the oldest. This is "the sacrifice of the Lord's passover, for he passed over the houses of the people of Israel in Egypt, when he slew the Egyptians but spared our houses" (Exod. 12:27). This event is not sealed in the past. This is "our" story, alive in present obedient practice.

Due to the complexities of the Jewish lunar calendar, Christian observance of Holy Week will only correspond occasionally with Passover. Modern non-Jewish Christians must understand why Jews often feel dismay at Christian Passover seders. This story establishes the distinctive identity of Israel. How dare gentile Christians also lay claim to it?

The problem is as deep as the biblical witness to God's election of Israel, and the New Testament explicitly cautions gentile Christians against boasting against the Jews (see Romans 11:13-27). Nevertheless, this story is also "our" Christian story because of its fulfillment by the Messiah and Lamb of God, Jesus.

Above all, this story proclaims the mighty saving act of God. This day is commanded to be kept as "a memorial day," as "a feast to the Lord; throughout your generations" (v. 14) because of what God has done. The Christian believer will recognize the "gospel logic" of this observance. The ritual is not meticulously observed "in order to" influence God or prove worthy. The point of remembrance is thanksgiving and trust.

What kind of God do we meet in Jesus Christ? This is the God who brought Israel out of slavery, championing their cause against the mighty Pharaoh. This is also the God who instituted a feast of remembrance so that even the children of future generations could experience the anticipation and bond of a people moving out in freedom. Every detail is filled with meaning, distinguishing this night from all other nights, inviting songs and prayers and shared memories. This is a God who intends to stay involved with the families and community of a people. The Passover and exodus are only the beginning.

The Christian reader knows that this God has instituted yet another feast for the faithful. Once again, the meal is a remembrance of God's mighty redemption in the face of the forces of oppression and death. And this night, Maundy Thursday, is different from all other nights because of the Passover which Jesus celebrated. The profound ritual of the Passover provides the setting in which God's saving purpose is decisively revealed.

EPISTLE: 1 CORINTHIANS 11:17-32

Text: Several lectionaries for Holy Week include only vv. 23-26 in this reading from 1 Corinthians. In those verses, Paul recites the tradition that he received and previously transmitted to the Corinthians concerning the supper. His explicit reference to the tradition of Jesus' words and ritual is a historical treasure since it may be confidently identified as a memory piece which predates Paul's letters. It is also one of the very few Pauline references to a word of Jesus, providing a complex point of comparison to the "words of institution" as conveyed in Matt. 26:26-29, Mark 14:22-25, and Luke 22:14-20.

Scholars have been fascinated with Paul's affirmation that he received this tradition "from the Lord." In Gal. 1:12, he is intent on his claim that he did not receive his gospel "from a human, nor was I taught it, but it came through a revelation of Jesus Christ." This statement about the supper tradition also seems to fit that emphasis, but this "revelation" refers to a historical event of a meal at which others were present. What then is the connection between the tradition Paul received "from the Lord" and the church's memory of the supper?

This is not a huge historical problem since the Synoptic accounts agree as much with Paul as with each other. But it is an interesting insight into "revealed" and "received" tradition in earliest Christianity. Paul's interpretation of the supper is not based solely on an account whose accuracy can be verified historically, by consulting eyewitnesses. He claims its authenticity more in terms of the revelation he has received from the risen Lord. The meaning of the supper is not merely a matter of the historical record. Whatever historical memories were available to him, Paul proclaimed the gospel of the supper on the authority of revelation.

Paul is probably not challenging historical memory, but he is declaring its revealed significance. His own authority as an apostle is laid on the line for community concerns. What he has previously told them about the supper now authorizes his correction of their practice, and he proceeds on the authority of Christ. The risen Lord continues to be concerned with the supper's appropriate celebration.

In vv. 23-26, therefore, the words and ritual of the supper are neither mere memories nor magical incantations. Paul understands the risen Lord Jesus to be the revealer of his own supper. His command to "do this . . . in remembrance of me" anticipates more than reminiscence. The disciples of Epicurus may have been content with annual observances of the founder's birthday in the wake of his death. Jesus' disciples cannot settle for recalling the past.

Obedient "remembrance of me" also moves the faithful away from magical efforts to use the "words of institution" or "eucharistic actions" to affect God or alter the cosmos. When "remembrance" becomes an assertion of will, it perverts the promise and gospel of what God is doing into another human method of control. Since this is the *Lord's* supper and not a mere human feast, everything points to what the Lord Jesus has done. The "remembrance of me" is the link of faith and trust that the Lord has provided to the saving events. The risen Lord Jesus is Paul's witness that the observance of this supper is a means to "proclaim the Lord's death until he comes."

Paul may well have depended upon common Christian memories to know the historical words Jesus spoke on the night he was betrayed. But the tradition he conveyed to the Corinthians had apprehended the past in the light of the resurrection. The supper's proper place is now as a ritual of anticipation, an occasion of instruction and proclamation. The supper identifies and directs the community to its mission until the parousia.

In the larger context of vv. 17-32, therefore, Paul uses the common heritage of the meal to make an ethical point. He is bold to point out the Corinthians' abuse of the supper, holding them accountable to the will and judgment of the Lord. These are not finely tuned comments on liturgical particulars, as if a celebrant might be struck dead for mispronouncing the sacred words or a participant might be condemned for lack of understanding. No, Paul is addressing community relationships which are incompatible with the Lord's purposes in the supper.

Proclamation: The holiness of the God of the Bible is manifest in justice and mercy. The "noise of solemn assemblies" will not suffice for faithful worship, no matter how religiously proper it seems. Nor are God's saving acts merely another excuse for a party. The meal rituals of Passover and the Lord's supper resist normal human tendencies to coopt them. God and the Messiah Jesus have agenda and purpose in these rituals, and the biblical accounts are unusually directive and instructive for the faithful.

In the church, the temptation is always to turn God's saving act into our religious enterprise. Christian history includes lengthy discussions about "discerning the body" and eating and drinking "in an unworthy manner." Many of these deliberations are focused upon correct understanding or adequate human virtue, as if the efficacy of the supper depended upon our theology or morality. Certainly these human activities are significant since the effect of the Lord's supper on the unrepentant could be judgment rather than grace.

Nevertheless, the "discernment" of which Paul is speaking is not a matter of an arcane understanding of the two natures of Christ. Nor is Paul's caution about the "unworthy manner" directed at those who know they are unworthy. The hazard is greatest for those who presume that the supper is their personal right and thus disregard the whole body of the community. This is the *Lord's* supper, established by the Lord Jesus to sustain and instruct the church in its mission. Those who would use the meal to establish their religious domination or personal prerogatives will face the judgment of the Lord himself.

These perils are only understood within the church. The rest of the world is disinterested in Maundy Thursday and Holy Week, and certainly senses no awe or dread at not discerning the body of Christ in the supper. The bunnies, candy, and Easter bonnets have seized the attention of the public.

The rituals of "me first" always have greater economic value, and that party has already begun. Paul's witness to the reality of the Messiah's presence in the supper will shock those who thought they could simply use the meal to further their own religious agenda, and it will caution the church against observing the supper in contexts where its profound significance may be trivialized.

The discipline of Maundy Thursday is, therefore, instruction for believers. Historically the church reserved these rites for its baptized members, just as Israel restricted the Passover celebrations to the family. These are the deeper mysteries of the faith, requiring Christian communities to examine themselves and to listen to the word and will of the Lord Jesus.

Paul observed a congregation where some people were filling their plates from their abundance, and others had a few drinks before they even arrived. Perhaps none of them had stopped in the shopping mall to pick up an Easter outfit on their way to services, but the effect was the same. The ritual of the meal had been turned into a festival which perverted God's saving purpose.

Everyone wants to take the heritage of the faith and turn it into something else. The television accounts of Holy Week dwell on Ukrainian Easter eggs and festivals of parades and hunts. Many Christians are so conditioned by all of this that they only want happy rituals, encouraging all of us to reach our individual fulfillment. "Proclaiming the Lord's death until he comes" seems negative or abrasive.

Paul knows that the story of the Lord's supper is a mighty lesson in God's saving purpose in Christ Jesus. Even the words of institution will frustrate our attempts to use the meal for institutional control of God's grace. They will also challenge the trite religions of self-indulgence.

But they will touch the deepest nerve of human need, because the body of Christ Jesus has been broken "for you," and "this cup is the new covenant in my blood." The salvation they proclaim is the work of God, for us and for the world. We cannot seize control or turn this feast to our own purposes without perverting it and depriving ourselves of its benefit. But we can understand that the Messiah instituted the feast as an observance of his impending death. He is now raised and exalted, extending his saving reign through the obedient observance of his feast.

The real presence of Christ in the supper is not some metaphysical puzzle. It is the presence of the power and wisdom of God. The body and blood of the Messiah are announced in the words of institution, and all those who partake in the meal are confronted with the authority and grace of God's kingdom.

GOSPEL: JOHN 13:1-17, 34

Text: Chapter 13 marks a significant transition in John's narrative. Chapters 2–12 presented God's Son and Messiah in relationship to the world and humanity. Now "his hour had come to depart out of this world to the Father, having loved his own who were in the world" (13:1). Chapter 13 introduces Jesus' teaching (chaps. 14–17) before his arrest, trial, execution, and resurrection, and the narrative becomes noticeably more attentive to Jesus' relationship with God's heavenly realm.

In chap. 13, John portrays Jesus as fully knowing what is happening among his disciples and the relationship of all of this to God's purposes. The tension is sharp between Jesus' love of his disciples and his betrayal by one of them. Furthermore, the reader is privy to all of this knowledge, but the disciples only know in part. Consider these examples: "Jesus knew that his hour had come" (v. 1); "Jesus knowing that the Father had given all things into his hands. . ." (v. 3); "What I am doing you do not know now, but afterward you will understand" (v. 7); "For he knew who was to betray him" (v. 11); "If you know these things, blessed are you if you do them" (v. 17).

Jesus is the Lord and Teacher (v. 14) who instructs the disciples, past and present, in what they must know. He is calm and controlled, although terrible developments are taking place. The intrigue, betrayal, and confusion mount as the story unfolds, but neither Jesus nor the reader have cause for alarm. The forces of evil and chaos may appear to have the upper hand. In reality, "the Father had given all things into his hands . . . he had come from God and was going to God" (v. 3).

The depth of his instruction is revealed in his washing the feet of his disciples. This is not only a shocking challenge to authority structures, reversing the roles between servant and teacher; it is also stunning in the face of the impending crisis. How can footwashing be such a significant act for the Messiah to perform in his last hours with his disciples?

Footwashing is a cleansing ritual. Washing was an important religious activity in Israel because purification and pollution had dramatic consequences in the presence of God's holiness. Ancient religious traditions commonly practiced washing rituals for reasons of purification which were understood to be much more profound than hygiene.

Now Jesus washes his disciples' feet, knowing that a grave pollution lies ahead, bonding them to him in purity even before the betrayal. Peter's first objection against allowing the Lord to wash his feet turns into a plea to be washed head to foot. But the Lord indicates that this footwashing will suffice for cleansing all of them "all over," except for the betrayer.

This washing is accomplishing more than cleansing. In vv. 12-17, Jesus lets them "know what I have done to you." Jesus interprets this ritual of purification as instruction in discipleship. This is a lesson in the authority relationships of the community of the Messiah. As in the Passover story in the Old Testament lesson, the ritual is not finally a means for making the participants right with God or for appeasing God. The ritual is a divinely instituted instruction in God's will and reign.

Jesus identifies himself as their "Lord and Teacher" (v. 13). As such, his instruction has authority, even as it undermines customary authoritarian relationships. He is intent on teaching that his footwashing does not diminish his authority, but reveals his strength, grounded in his identity as servant.

Jesus teaches his disciples with authority, and his lesson instructs them in their proper authority and service. The teacher has a particular kind of authority in mind, distinct from usual understandings of power. Those who might fear their authority would be diminished by menial service of others must be taught.

Jesus will now enact his authority in the most profound way, walking knowingly into his death at the hands of those who think they control the power in the world. His view of authority is not merely his own. Jesus is operating on the authority of the one "who sent him" (v. 16). God sent the Son on an embassy of love, "not to condemn the world, but that the world might be saved through him" (3:17). Jesus' action displays God's strength and authority, fulfilled in love and service, to the point of death.

The Gospel text for Maundy Thursday thus reveals God's strangely powerful way of love through the act and word of the Teacher and Lord Jesus. The Messiah teaches this intentional lesson to interpret himself and to reveal God's purpose in sending him. God's ways are not those of the world, and the disciples of the Lord Jesus are now called to "know" and "do" what God has made known and done (v. 17). The lesson is consistent with the revelation of the entire Gospel.

This mundane ritual of cleansing and lesson in servant authority thus provides a significant glimpse into Jesus' relationship with the Father. The narrative brings the reader inside the ancient rituals of purification and offers an object lesson in authority. It also leads into a deeper grasp of Jesus' obedience to God's will, acknowledging his role as the one who is sent, while serving those to whom he is sent. The ultimate irony is that he washes the feet of the one who "lifted his heel against me," while knowing what will happen (vv. 16-18).

The power of the Messiah is revealed in his restraint and loving service. John's version of the arrest will emphasize that Jesus could have used his divine authority overtly, but he did not (18:4-6, 36; 19:10-11). The glorification that lies ahead is truly glorification, but it will occur through the elevation of the Son of man on the instrument of execution (13:31). God's mysterious salvation is being fulfilled in hidden strength.

Proclamation: Perhaps footwashing should be recognized as a sacrament along with Baptism and the Lord's Supper. The Lord's command to his disciples concerning footwashing is "that you also should do as I have done to you" (v. 15). In mainline churches, this ritual evokes embarrassment, just as it did among the disciples. Its challenge is inescapable. Who is the minister and who is in control? What kind of service is this and what does it imply about the one performing the act?

Loving mothers and fathers wash their children's ears, feet, and bottoms. Their ministry is of the humblest kind, but it does not diminish their stature. Their relationship of trust and parental responsibility are of one piece. Loving service and authority belong together. In many cultures, this care continues to the bathing and preparation of a body for burial. In modern settings, the bathing, turning, and care for hospice and AIDS patients have returned again to the hands of families and caring Christian congregations.

The Christian faith is so radically incarnate that believers must be washers and caregivers. Disembodied messages simply are not adequate to convey the strength and depth of God's love to those who need it. When Jesus washed his disciples' feet, he gave them an object lesson in ministerial authority, demonstrating the depth of his authorization from God. That is significant to his role as a Servant Messiah. But he also commanded them to continue doing the same because this is God's way of loving and caring for flesh and blood people like us.

Anne Dillard speaks of humans as "flesh flecks" in the vast reaches of the universe. God knows that we are frail flesh, and God has met us in the flesh in the person of Jesus Christ. God does not merely love our "souls," as if we were disembodied spirits. Jesus wraps himself in a towel and washes the dirt of Palestine from between his disciples' toes.

Ritual gives meaning to life whether in threat or promise. Our daily routines of a morning shower, brushing our teeth, and evening bedtime preparations involve more than personal appearance or hygiene. These are marks of good order, and they measure our control of our affairs. When we are no longer able to do these things for ourselves, the order of our lives passes into the hands of others.

Christians have long marked the beginning and end of the day with prayers of repentance and thanksgiving. These spiritual exercises are like the rituals of the flesh, ordering the time and marking its meaning. Bedtime bathing and prayer are all wrapped together in loving homes. The body and the spirit are not separated, and those who do these things for us in our infancy or infirmity sustain our worth and convey God's love to us. Their authority is never in question.

The counsel of despair insists that "life is just one damn thing after another and then you die." The cynics and those whose hopes have been crushed agree on this lamentable verdict. Even the story of Jesus' betrayal and death could be interpreted as the triumph of chaos. Pilate would not have regarded the Passover meal or the washing of the disciples' feet by this Lord and Master as significant at all. Perhaps even Judas had concluded that this deluded Messiah was about to be executed.

But Jesus washed his disciples' feet in the face of his impending betrayal and death. The homey ritual was probably grounded in practices of hospitality for guests and travelers, and the Messiah attended to such human detail in the midst of the central drama of history. Jesus was never so busy saving the world that he forgot to serve.

Those who bring food in the time of a death and those who visit the sick with the sacrament in Holy Week understand this same reality. Care and love are conveyed in the humblest human ways. No form of service is beneath the Christian because none was too low for the Messiah.

A woman who spent years caring for abandoned and abused children in the slums of the world was asked how she could do it. She had watched hundreds of children die of malnutrition when her United Nations resources had come too late or run out, but she had also bravely built health care and educational facilities to save countless others. "Every day," she said, "I remembered the Christlike faith of my mother and father. The only way I survived was to cling to that faith for myself."

God's strategy to save the world is humble and strong. The service which the Messiah renders his disciples in washing their feet is not a sentimental display. It is a fundamental revelation of the authority and power of the kingdom of God. Jesus is not merely teaching his disciples a lesson in humility. He is inducting them into the mystery of God's righteous rule perfected in mercy.

The body and blood of the Lord Jesus are broken and shed "for you" (see the epistle lesson), and the Messiah who washes his disciples' feet is about to be elevated to reign from a cross. This is not the theater of the absurd. The evangelist and the Messiah know that God's saving power is at work.

There is time and reason to wash feet and teach the disciples because nothing more important is happening than God's care and love for these mere mortals. No one is more important in the kingdom of God than the one who needs love and care. This is the mystery, revelation, and hope of the drama of Holy Week.

Good Friday

Lutheran	Roman Catholic	Episcopal	Common Lectionary
Isa. 52:13—53:12	Isa. 52:13—53:12	Isa. 52:13—53:12	Isa. 52:13—53:12
Heb. 4:14-16; 5:7-9	Heb. 4:14-16; 5:7-9	Heb. 10:1-25	Heb. 4:14-16; 5:7-9
John 18:1—19:42 *or* John 19:17-30	John 18:1—19:42	John 19:1-37	John 18:1—19:42 *or* John 19:17-30

Collect for Good Friday: Almighty God, we ask you to look with mercy on your family, for whom our Lord Jesus Christ was willing to be betrayed and to be given over to the hands of sinners and to suffer death on the cross; who now lives and reigns with you and the Holy Spirit, one God, forever and ever. Amen.

FIRST LESSON: ISAIAH 52:13—53:12

Text: The fourth "servant song" of Isaiah 40–55 has been subject to intense study by ancient and modern interpreters. The early Christians found this passage to be a script for the brutal humiliation, execution, and vindication of Jesus, testifying profoundly to the expiatory character of Jesus' innocent suffering and death. It will be impossible to read this passage in the context of Good Friday without sensing its immense power for interpreting the meaning of Jesus' passion.

Modern historical scholarship, however, has reminded readers that this servant song had its own historical occasion in Israel, long before the birth of Jesus. This reminder has caused some consternation among both Christians and Jews, since a more strict historical interpretation raises questions about what subsequent generations have seen in the passage. Some interpreters have even declared all "messianic" use of the text illegitimate, as if "what it meant" in Isaiah's time was its only valid usage.

The historical meaning of the passage certainly deserves special attention. It is instructive to consider the specific human and historical occasion(s) to which it was first addressed.

This powerful poetic piece or parts of it probably predate the writing of these chapters in Isaiah. The cycle of "songs of the servant" in Isaiah has impressive coherence (see also 42:1-4; 49:1-6; 50:4-11). The ease with which these songs can be lifted from their literary context has prompted careful study of their distinctive message. But even if the songs had another origin, their message is now thoroughly integrated into the prophet's witness in these chapters.

The larger context is an extended testimony to the strength and triumph of God's reign in the restoration of Israel. Isaiah 40–55 is one of the Bible's most affirmative statements of God's mighty dominion in human history. The prophet and the Word of God sing in chorus, proclaiming the God of Israel as the true Lord in human affairs. All the other gods and rulers are idols and errand runners for the Lord. And Israel's return has vindicated God's mighty rule. Now the "waste places of Jerusalem" may "break forth together into singing . . . for the Lord has comforted his people, he has redeemed Jerusalem . . . and all the ends of the earth shall see the salvation of our God" (52:9-10).

But "Jacob my servant, Israel whom I have chosen" (44:1) is not so evidently powerful or glorious. God has dealt harshly with Israel in captivity, and in return this servant's exaltation will be a revelation of God's salvation at work in the suffering of Israel. The logic is the same as the deuteronomic witness to Moses the servant of God who suffers on behalf of his people.

The suffering servant Israel "shall startle many nations; kings shall shut their mouths because of him" (52:15). The saving reign of God is revealed to the whole world in the vindication of this unlikely servant, and his suffering thus produces salvation from their sin: "and with his stripes we are healed."

This song recalls the reality of Israel's suffering even as the glory of the restoration becomes evident. The servant who returns still bears scars, and they bear witness to God's restoration of a sinful people and salvation of the world. The dire suffering of this people reveals the strength of the salvation which God is determined to accomplish. "It is too light a thing that you should be my servant . . . to restore the tribes of Jacob . . . I will give you as a light to the nations that my salvation may reach to the end of the earth" (49:6).

The prophet is interpreting Israel's return from exile as a revelation of divine judgment and salvation. The message is directed first to Israel, but the entire gallery of nations and rulers observes and overhears. This one servant has borne "the iniquity of us all" (53:6). The divine plan of restoration is full of remembrance of one who "was taken away . . . by oppression and judgment" (53:8), who was "numbered with the transgressors; yet he bore the sin of many, and made intercession for the transgressors" (53:12).

Israel never ceased to be God's chosen servant, even in exile. Nor had God abandoned the determination to bless all the nations through the blessing of the offspring of Abraham. Even through Israel's suffering in exile, God sustained this intention to save, and Israel's role was exercised through humiliation.

Proclamation: The prophet is already preaching to Israel and the nations. "This is how God has been at work in Israel's history. This is how God's strength is perfected through sinful and weak human instruments. Do not mistake God's faithful bond with Israel for folly or the suffering of the servant for God's weakness. And do not imagine that it is easy for a human people to be God's chosen servant."

The mystery of Holy Week is captured in the poetry of the prophet. He was speaking to his times, seeking to understand and declare God's saving purpose in the agony of Israel's exile and surprise of her restoration. Even then, not everything was glorious. The past could not be discarded, and the future seemed uncertain. Was this merely an arbitrary reversal of fortune? Could Israel hope in the future? Could God be trusted?

Not only did the prophet reassure his people, without any trivial consolations, but with this song he also gathered up a rich biblical witness to God's saving ways with a sinful people. Neither the suffering nor the hope were diminished. These experiences were both affirmed within God's purposes. How else could the God who intends to establish a reign of true justice and mercy work through the chosen human servant Israel?

And what passage could better supply the script for Jesus and the early Christian community to enact and understand God's ultimate saving purpose? Certainly the knowledge of this text must be assumed for the earliest accounts of Jesus' death and resurrection. The details of Jesus' grave with "a rich man in his death" and being "numbered among the transgressors" are more than brute facts in the Passion story. They are links into the plan of God, revealing that Jesus' humiliation and death were part of the divine plan. This fit with what God had been doing all along.

The Isaiah text has its power apart from the story of Jesus. To say that Jesus' death is a fulfillment of this prophecy does not diminish the force of the prophecy itself in its address to Israel returning from exile. The Isaiah prophecy is a word of God even for those in Israel who do not believe in Jesus.

But for those who confess Jesus to be God's Messiah and Servant par excellence, this prophecy identifies and confirms God's will and plan fulfilled in Jesus. God's will to accomplish the promised saving reign has never wavered, and even God's way has been made known through the law and the prophets. What God wrought in part through the servant people Israel has now been perfected in the suffering and death of the one who was truly innocent and without violence.

EPISTLE: HEBREWS 4:14-16; 5:7-9

Text: The book of Hebrews offers a glimpse into a distinctive first century world of Jewish and Christian thought. The sustained arguments from the psalms and worship traditions of Israel are unmatched in the New Testament. The "many and various ways" through which God had spoken through the prophets in the past stand in contrast to God's word "to us by a Son" in the person of Jesus (1:1-2).

The arguments are not always easy to follow. They presume a religious subculture of scriptural interpretation in which the temple cult and its sacrifices are thoroughly understood. Jesus has been "designated by God a high priest after the order of Melchizedek" (5:10) as well as the exalted Son to whom divine rule has been entrusted (see 1:5, 5:5). Jesus' identity and role may not be taken for granted. Scriptural commentary and interpretation of Israel's temple practices must undergird Christian trust in Jesus as the pioneer and perfecter of faith.

The lesson for Good Friday draws upon some of the rich poetry of the testimony of Hebrews, but the selections ignore the argumentation. By omitting 5:1-6 and 5:10, the context of these powerful words of assurance has been lost. Perhaps the omission is necessary since the argument is strange to modern ears, and references to the "high priest after the order of Melchizedek" sound impossibly arcane. But now the affirmations about Jesus sound merely like commendations of his character (e.g. able "to sympathize with our weakness," . . . "he learned obedience through what he suffered; and being made perfect he became the source of eternal salvation"). For Hebrews these statements are declarations of the status which God has conferred upon him.

The point is that God designated Jesus for a unique high priesthood, accomplishing the perfection of which the human cultus was not capable. The temple in Jerusalem was not evil, but it was only an earthly copy of the heavenly reality. In the Platonic cosmology of Hebrews and the Hellenistic world, no earthly replica could hope for heavenly perfection. Thus no priestly tradition or cultic practices could escort sinful humanity through the heavenly courts.

The suffering and death of Jesus were thus the ultimate divine act of condescension, of a "Son" both "sympathizing with our weakness" and "learning obedience through what he suffered." This is radical talk, not about Jesus' personality, but about God's plan to bridge the gap between heavenly perfection and the human plight. The very idea that the heavenly "Son" could "learn" through suffering was a profound affirmation of the reality of human life. God had entered into history with a risk and vulnerability that the Platonists would have thought heresy.

Hebrews lays a heavy stress on Jesus' humanity. He was "tempted" or "tested in every respect as we are, yet without sin." His "loud cries and tears" were not affectations of a divine being who was actually unthreatened

by death. Jesus redeemed human temptation, suffering, and earthly exist-
ence by undergoing the entire subjection.

His exaltation or "being made perfect," therefore, had saving effect for
mere mortals. This was not merely a display of an unattainable ideal. This
was a rescue mission through which the "Son" and "High Priest after the
order of Melchizekek" became "the source of eternal salvation to all who
obey him" (5:9).

Proclamation: The Hebrews text is in danger of becoming a mere adorn-
ment of Good Friday. When the argument of the book is snipped away by
the scissors of the editors of the lectionary, the affirmations which remain
sound merely like priestly praise. Jesus is to be admired and emulated. He
is a model of perfection inviting obedience. The rich word of evangelical
hope of Hebrews may be perverted into a new demand of perfection or
reduced to a heap of ritualistic phrases.

But the gospel word is central to Hebrews. Our confidence in drawing
"near to the throne of grace" (4:16) is grounded in what Jesus has done.
We could not face every test without sinning, and Hebrews is particularly
sensitive to the sin of apostasy from faith in Jesus. We know that God's
reign is exercised from "the throne of grace" because Jesus is the one
seated on it, and this Jesus has the salvation that we need because he has
been here in all respects. We could never aspire to such perfection. Our
hope and salvation lie in Jesus who has pioneered and perfected our faith
by what he has done.

Many first- and twentieth-century religions have objected to the Christian
faith on the grounds that a suffering "Son of God" could never be divine.
The idea that Jesus would "learn" or make progress or become perfect
through suffering was simply unworthy of spiritual consideration. Hebrews
was not only a direct challenge to the ancient Platonists, but it also serves
now as a sharp prod against many modern religious sensibilities, from
Christian science, to new age spiritualities, to Mormonism. The priestly
perfection of Jesus is anchored in the "once for all" suffering (9:26) of
this "Son" and "high priest after the order of Melchizedek."

Good Friday insists on the scandal of particularity. The whole drama of
heaven and earth comes down to Jesus. He is not another avatar, another
teacher, another priest. The relationship of heaven and earth is redefined
in Jesus. Even common conceptions of sin, salvation, and perfection have
new meanings in the light of Jesus' suffering and exaltation.

The Son and High Priest to whom we pray has nail-scarred hands. He
is not less than the angels for having experienced and learned the painful
lessons of mortal humanity. The whole order of heaven, rather, is held in

awe by this one whom God has exalted. The deepest mystery of the universe is permeated with the light of Jesus' ascent. The overwhelming distances are overcome between earth and heaven, between mortal and heavenly realms, between sinful humanity and the perfection of divine holiness.

The sixth-century Easter hymn of Venantius Honorius Fortunatus declares this same gospel:

> Praise the Savior, now and ever;
> Praise him all beneath the skies;
> Come before him and adore him,
> God's own perfect sacrifice;
> Victr'y gaining, life obtaining,
> Now in glory see him rise!
> (*Lutheran Book of Worship* 155)

God had this in mind all along, and Jesus prevailed in God's favor to accomplish it. No detail of the execution of this "Son" and "High Priest" is insignificant. Every glimpse of his perfect obedience in the midst of loud cries and bitter tears is a revelation of divine grace. This is the salvation that God has created in the midst of the earth because it is God's purpose to save earthlings like us.

GOSPEL: JOHN 18:1—19:42

Text: John's entire story of Jesus' arrest, trials before Caiaphas and Pilate, execution, and burial should be read together. This narrative forms a coherent basis for a Good Friday "tenebrae service" in place of the seven last words. John's account includes a larger arena than "stations of the cross," leading the hearer into the struggle of wills and authorities surrounding Jesus' death. The culmination of this struggle is the ironic execution of "the King of the Jews." Even if time constraints in the service will only allow reading John 19:17-30 aloud, the preacher will do well to consider this account of Jesus' death within the larger passage.

The shorter reading includes three of the traditional "seven last words": "Woman, behold your son! . . . Behold your mother!" (19:26-27); "I thirst" (19:28); and "It is finished" (19:30). Taken together these words plumb the depths of Jesus' human anguish, but without a hint of despair. John offers more than a glimpse into Jesus' psyche. This is a revelation of the control and obedience unto death of the exalted Jesus. Even his cry of thirst is spoken "to fulfill the scripture" of Psalm 69:21.

Jesus is regal in every measure. This is what the Son of man "lifted up" looks like (see 3:14; 8:28; 12:34). The central mystery of Jesus' death lies hidden and revealed in the title above his head written in three languages, "Jesus of Nazareth, the King of the Jews."

The larger narrative indicates the meaning of this charge and title, but it also presents the modern reader with a extreme difficulty. How can this bizarre inscription be understood as anything but anti-Judaism? Almost two millennia of anti-Semitic Christian preaching cannot be ignored, and the problem of "the Jews" in John's Gospel resists easy solutions. Nevertheless, a few observations may be helpful.

First of all, all of the Gospels were written in a time when most of the Christians were Jewish. The conflicts between "Judeans" and "Messianists" persisted even when the Judeans (or Jews) were Christian, as is evident in Acts 15 and Galatians. The term "the Jews" in John is filled with complex associations that are now very difficult to unravel historically. Suffice it to say that even its most pejorative sense (as in 19:12) probably reflects conflict among Christians as well as between Jewish parties. This is the language of a family fight. John could not know that later generations of "gentile" Christians would use these words against "the Jews."

Secondly, Pilate and the Roman soldiers are playing a complex game of taunt and abuse with Jesus and also with the Jewish leaders. The exchange between Jesus and Pilate in John 18 presents the procurator as interrogating the accused as to whether he is "the King of the Jews" and protesting ignorance with mock innocence, "Am I a Jew?" Neither Jesus nor the religious leaders assert that he is "The King of the Jews," but the soldiers (19:3) and Pilate (18:33, 39; 19:14-15, 19-22) insist on the title which is also a charge.

Something is going on here which is deeper than either politics or blame. The religious leaders in Israel and Pilate are caught in a web beyond their own weaving. Their arrogance is evident, but their arrogant proclamation of "Jesus of Nazareth, the King of the Jews" is a profound revelation of the truth.

Pilate's words are a charge against both Jesus and the Jews because only the Roman senate or emperor could declare anyone "King of the Jews." Judea was a Roman province, and Herod the Great was the last king to be granted this title. His descendants dearly wanted such official Roman recognition, but now the province was being governed by a procurator. By insisting on this charge, Pilate intends to let all Judea know who is in charge here and what becomes of royal pretenders.

The evangelist, however, invites the reader to wonder about who is finally in charge in this strange scene. The verdict and sentence are Pilate's. But after he has baited the crowd, does he truly want to kill Jesus? His question, "What is truth?" (18:38), sounds weary or cynical in the midst of the grave issues at stake. Even when Pilate insists that he is allowing an innocent man to die and seems to try to release him, the crowd reveals his weakness before intimidation. If refusing to execute Jesus would imperil his standing before Caesar, what will become of a procurator who yields to the will of the mob? So, who is in charge? Is it the mob? Or are both Pilate and the crowd tyrannized by Caesar in Rome? Where does ultimate power lie?

For those with the eyes to see, God's will and reign are being established in these strange events. The reader need not wonder with Pilate about the truth, because the faithful witness who "saw" what happened told the truth and knew he told it (19:35), and the Scriptures confirm this witness (19:36). This scene is the fulfillment of God's promise and reign.

The evangelist knows all about the facts of history, but the factors of history are still more significant. Yes, Jesus died with the religious leadership of his own people jeering him on. Yes, the Roman procurator vacillated and relinquished his rule to the mob. All of the mighty claims of Rome to divine legitimacy ring hollow in Pilate's sarcastic verdict.

But the charge above Jesus' head speaks God's truth. Jesus of Nazareth is being confirmed as God's ruler in Israel. This is not merely a divine strategy to condemn the world, although Israel and Rome are implicated. This is the fulfillment of God's determined will to save the world.

The hope of Jew and Greek, all sinful humanity, lies in this crucified Messiah. The evangelist tells the frightening story not to vindicate one group at the expense of another. That is exactly the mistake of anti-Judaism. Rather the terror and tragic blindness become revelations, disclosures of divine grace because God's saving will, the fulfillment of the scriptural promises, is truly at work.

Finally God's will is done in this story, not Pilate's, not "the Jews", not Peter's or the other disciples'. Only in the retrospect of Easter is God's will evident. The blindness and tragic insistence on their own will confirm that those who call for Jesus' death merely condemn themselves. But no later reader, Christian, Roman, or Jew, can claim superiority. God's justification silences all human boasting.

Proclamation: The only good thing about "Good Friday" is the salvation God accomplished in the midst of human sin. There is no virtue in this story, except the obedience of the crucified Messiah. The dignity of the dying King of the Jews is a glimpse for believing eyes of the glorious reign which God promised in Israel's Scriptures, but only the faithful can see hope in Jesus' death.

For those who confidently "explain" Jesus' death in merely psychological or political terms, John's story is shocking. Paul's sermon in Acts sounds a similar warning in the words of Habakkuk: "Behold, you scoffers, and wonder, and perish; for I do a deed in your days, a deed you will never believe, if one declares it to you" (Hab. 1:5; Acts 13:41).

This text catches the wise in their craftiness and brings down the mighty. It allows no superiority. Those who are confident that divine might and right are on their side could never accept God's incredible freedom and grace in the reign of the crucified Messiah. The Roman procurator and his soldiers smirked and jeered. The local leaders gasped in theological superiority, and the followers of the Messiah fought futilely and despaired. No one could keep pace with God's strange and gracious way of exalting Jesus to reign.

Perhaps only the outcasts can understand, only the AIDS patients, or the parents of a child who died of cancer. Maybe those who have come face-to-face with their profound sin or had their shame exposed could know. The story of Jesus' death is a radical remedy for a sickness unto death, nothing less.

A pastor in South Africa told of months in solitary confinement. He had been taken, without trial, brutally beaten, subjected to electric shock all over his naked body until the burns seared every movement, every function. Again and again he was told that all had abandoned him. He was the enemy of the people, the heretic, the communist hated by God.

Praying for death on a concrete floor smeared with his blood, he saw Jesus come to him. The pierced hands, the wounded side, the crown of thorns were all intact. The only word was, "I am with you." Whether he lived or died was no longer the question. He even dared once again to pray to live.

Christians have long prayed to be "washed in the blood." This is more than a metaphor. It is an affirmation of hope in God, of trust in the salvation which God wrought through the bloody death of the Messiah Jesus.

The pouring out of Jesus' life, of his blood, is a tale of terror. The horror is compounded by the fact that the religious leaders, the crowd, and the Roman procurator thought they were justified or at least excused in their deed by higher considerations. Jesus did not die a bloodless, quiet death in a sanctuary. He was executed in public among other victims of Roman justice in occupied Israel.

But this Jesus was and is God's king, the true King of the Jews by divine decree. He fulfilled the scriptural promises, and God turned human violence and scorn into the means of life and hope. Because God is at work in this story, because this is God's will being done, Jesus' death is the sign and promise of life.

The preacher's task is to bring this home, to tell this dire tale in a way that touches the deepest human need. The grace and mercy of God can never be cool or bloodless because this is a story of bloody passion, of love for flesh-and-blood people like those who assemble to hear once again. The word of the Lord for them is, "Jesus poured out his blood for you."

Only glimpses of this sure hope are given in the story. The bitter sarcasm and taunts seem to prevail. If Easter hope were not secure, there would be nothing "good" about Good Friday. Furthermore, true Easter joy never diminishes the stark reality of this trial, execution, and death. The depth of the hope of Easter is measured in the profound mystery of Jesus' shameful death.

But for those with eyes to see, this "King of the Jews" is truly God's ruler and our savior. No shame, no pain, no abandonment can be beyond his dominion. The good news of Good Friday extends to all who cling only to Christ and his righteousness. This is the ruler who has fulfilled the saving purposes of God.

Easter Vigil

Lutheran	Roman Catholic	Episcopal	Common Lectionary
Gen. 1:1—2:3	Gen. 1:1—2:2	Gen. 1:1—2:2	Gen. 1:1—2:2
Gen. 22:1-18	Gen. 22:1-18	Gen. 22:1-18	Gen. 22:1-18
Exod. 14:10—15:1	Exod. 14:10—15:1	Exod. 14:10—15:1	Exod. 14:10—15:1
Isa. 55:1-11	Isa. 55:1-11	Isa. 55:1-11	Isa. 55:1-11
Col. 3:1-4	Rom. 6:3-11	Rom. 6:3-11	Rom. 6:3-11
Matt. 28:1-10	Matt. 28:1-10	Matt. 28:1-10	Matt. 28:1-10

The ancient rite of the Easter Vigil is a sequel to the measured march of the Messiah to death. The deed has been done, both in what humanity has done to Jesus and in what Jesus has accomplished. This is the time to watch and wait, a sustained pause filled with expectation of God's mighty Easter vindication.

By tradition, this is not a time for preaching but for listening to the scriptural word of God. Perhaps some words of meditation may surround the readings. Certainly a worship service which is built around these passages will reflect their movement from the creation of the world to the dim light of Easter morning. The hymns, prayers, rituals, and testimony will not be rushed, but neither will this midnight meeting be aimless. The watching and waiting of the Easter Vigil focus upon God's mighty acts, God's saving acts reaching the climax of history.

Notice the grand sweep of these passages, and observe the dramatic shift away from the historical particularity of the preceding Gospel lessons. The intensity and anguish of the passion narratives have receded. Exactly why Pilate allowed the will of the mob or which was Jesus' last word are now matters of memory. All these things have become historical puzzles. We ponder these questions in the retrospect of Jesus' death, but our attention is no longer riveted on such specifics.

The rhythm and tone of the vigil are familiar to all who have experienced the aftermath of death. Dear friends will sit with the family, sometimes through the night before the funeral. There is nothing to be done and plenty of time. Long readings, prayers, and silences are appropriate. The details of the burial are momentary concerns, but the slow pace supports the grieving, the letting go, the yielding to God that must take place.

The secret of this vigil, of course, has already been told. The resignation of a death watch has been altered by expectation. A knowing wink may betray all of the other somber faces in the congregation. As surely as dawn follows night, those who keep the vigil are already looking forward to the angel's announcement. They are brimming with the word, "He is risen."

The ancient church caught this spirit in the midnight baptisms of adult converts. The vigil is an ideal occasion for the renewal of the baptism of all Christians into the death and resurrection of Christ. This is still the hour to observe when "Christ Jesus lay in death's strong bands" and to consider the call to discipleship as induction into his death. But this observation is filled with the hope and confidence of the dawn which is about to break.

GENESIS 1:1—2:3

This passage is a brilliant selection for the first reading. It must not be neglected, and only a bare minimum of commentary should accompany it, if any comments are offered at all. But the reader should be instructed in the momentous quality of this first reading so that the text may be recited with understanding.

We begin at the beginning in this vigil, the beginning of the Bible and the beginning of the world. The death of Jesus is projected on the whole screen of creation since time began. Another time we will zoom in on our little moment of time, relate Jesus' death and resurrection to our lives. But first we will go back, sweeping through millennia to the creation of the cosmos, seeking the big picture, striving to comprehend the mind of God.

We listen patiently to the story of creation as told by a witness whom scholars call the "Priestly" writer. There is no hurry as day follows day, age follows age, and morning follows evening. The whole is divided into parts in a sevenfold week of ages until the sabbath rest of God. The order and goodness of the whole and its parts are profoundly reassuring, and the cadence of the story expresses this order. All things great and small are created good for the blessing of the world and its inhabitants, including the man and the woman.

From the beginning, God has had blessing in mind for humanity and creation. The world is not the creation of an evil demiurge or a casual concatenation of events. Maltbie Babcock's hymn says it well:

This is my Father's world,
Oh, let me not forget
That though the wrong seems oft so strong,
God is the ruler yet.

GENESIS 22:1-18

The story of the testing of Abraham is frightening, perhaps especially in this context when we need to be assured that God is not our adversary. The creation story affirmed God's gracious purpose and order in the world, and Isaac is the child of promise, born to Abraham and Sarah at a time when hope seemed vain. But the terror of God's command is reflected even in its repetition: "Take your son, your only son Isaac, whom you love, and go to the land of Moriah, and offer him there as a burnt offering upon one of the mountains of which I shall tell you."

The story is full of Isaac's innocent questions, Abraham's silence, and the ominous progress toward the sacrifice. Now the orderliness of the narrative conveys threat, not promise. Abraham's obedience is astonishing, but frightening too.

The story is finally a demonstration of God's mercy, intervening in Abraham's faithfulness before tragedy occurs. This is a testing of God, although Abraham never seemed to know it. The story proves God's faithfulness to the promise, reaffirming the confidence of the creation story in God's saving purpose.

The early Christian interpreters were fascinated with the fact that the Lord provided the offering in place of Abraham's son. They also stressed that God did not spare his own Son, Jesus, when he was offered up. They saw the death of Jesus as completing the sacrifice which Abraham was finally not required to make.

EXODUS 14:10—15:1

Once more the reading recalls a time of great peril and salvation. The Easter Vigil includes both the sweep of the ages and a rehearsal of climactic moments in the history of the people of God. Israel's crossing of the Red Sea is another dramatic intervention, complete with angelic agency.

This story is a lesson in God's triumph, which is celebrated briefly in 15:1. It is crucial to note that this triumph is not a blessing of imperial might, but the vindication of the faith of those who trust God's promises in the face of all odds. The key to the triumph lies in Moses' speech to the fearful Israelites in 14:13-14, and in God's declaration in 14:18. The salvation of Israel through the sea is a "theodicy," proving the righteous reign of God before the court of world opinion.

This is exactly the issue in the death of Jesus. Will God vindicate the faithful Servant-Messiah, thereby proving the ultimacy of God's kingdom which Jesus has proclaimed? It is noteworthy that Luke (9:31, see NEB) reports that on the mountain of transfiguration, Moses and Elijah had discussed with Jesus "the exodus which he was to fulfill in Jerusalem." The early Christians understood the crossing of the Red Sea as a baptism, anticipating Christian baptism into the death and resurrection of Jesus (1 Cor. 10:1-4). What God accomplished in the resurrection of Jesus was a new thing, but it was also consistent with earlier vindications of divine promise.

ISAIAH 55:1-11

The note of promise is as clear in this passage as any in the Bible. The assurance of God's triumph is as secure as the fruitfulness of God's word. This prophetic oracle declares God's distinct ways and saving purposes often in first person speech, quoting God.

This joyful hymn of triumph also declares the fulfillment of the complex process which the songs of the Servant have been announcing throughout Holy Week. Suffering and salvation have been inseparable, as they are in Good Friday and Easter. But now the prophet begins the song of Easter, even before the gray light of morning creeps above the horizon.

COLOSSIANS 3:1-4 and ROMANS 6:3-11

These are alternative readings in the lectionaries. Both emphasize the bond of the faithful to the death and resurrection of Christ. The fate of the disciple is inextricably bound to that of the Messiah, and the Easter hope pervades this relationship. These are briefer readings than the Old Testament narratives. Why not use both, beginning with Colossians?

The death and resurrection of Christ provide the basis for an ethical appeal in Colossians which is the point of vv. 1-2. Verses 3-4, however, state the evangelical faith, the matter of fact of our link with Christ. The future hope of unity in Christ's resurrected glory is anchored in this fact.

By the time this passage is read the entire congregation has already moved ahead to Easter. In fact, the consequences and promise of the resurrection of Jesus is already being explored. The vigil is breaking down but only because the Christian hope cannot be contained.

In Romans 6, the sequence of what has already been accomplished for Christ identifies where we are and may expect to be in the future. This is a passage for those who have already been baptized, now bonded into his death that is a past event for Christ and for us. But we are also thereby united with him who has already been raised, and thus our hope for resurrection is assured.

Paul concludes this reading with an ethical appeal, just as Colossians 4 begins. The point, however, is to declare the facts, the realities within which we now live. For the baptized, these are declarations of freedom from death and sin and of hope for life now and in the resurrection.

Even the intricacy of Paul's argument is a revelation of his confidence. This reading has pulled us far beyond the first joy of Easter morning, into a Christian rabbi's exploration of what it all means. That Christ Jesus was raised from the dead is already assured. Paul cannot wait to instruct us in the promise and hope which the resurrection holds for our lives.

MATTHEW 28:1-10

None of the evangelists tells us how Jesus was raised by God. Only Matthew even mentions the earthquake and the angel descending to roll away the stone. Furthermore, the Easter morning appearances of Jesus are extremely brief. Mark only tells of the appearance of the messenger in the tomb. John and Luke proceed with stories about the disciples' lack of recognition. All agree that Jesus was raised by God and that this resurrection was a stunning surprise to his disciples.

"He is not here; for he has risen" is the message that transforms the world. Everything is changed. The dread march from Passion Sunday to Golgotha has been turned into a celebration. That word that evokes fear and joy among the followers is the climax of the Easter Vigil. All that is left to say is, "Go tell!"

There will be time for elaboration, but not now. The slow pace of the vigil has shifted into a rush of activity. "Blow out the candles! The sun is up!" Or more critically, "Jesus Christ is risen today! Alleluia!"